WHAT OTHERS ARE SAYING ABOUT *BEYOND GUILT*

This book is amazing. I wish more churches in America could grasp its ideas of ministry. George Johnson challenges us to go beyond tossing a few coins to the homeless. His book is empowering and inspiring.

**Joel Roberts, American Baptist clergy and Executive Director
People Assisting the Homeless, Los Angeles**

George Johnson has done it again. Beyond Guilt is a wake up call for capturing once again important teachings of the Reformation. This is a must reading.

**C. Dean Freudenberger, Methodist, Clergy, Agronomist,
Missionary and Seminary Professor**

This book brings home the urgency reflected in an African saying, "When a person is hungry, tomorrow is a long way away." Johnson challenges and invites us to act today. He dares to open our eyes to what flows from the scriptures.

Kathryn Wolford, Executive Director, Lutheran World Relief

Beyond Guilt *reminds us that we are called to work in expectation of the better world God intends. This book is as timely and relevant as the first edition. I'm glad its out.*

David Beckmann, President, Bread for the World

What a gift George Johnson has given us by revising and expanding Beyond Guilt *and* Powerlessness. *The chapter on care of the creation is worth the price of the book.*

Karen Fitzpatrick, Catholic member, Bread for the World Board

Beyond Guilt *brings together that needed balance of the personal and the social, the evangelical and the prophetic, the biblical and the life-situational. Few have done this as well at Johnson has in this marvelous contribution to the whole church.*

Lowell Erdahl, Bishop Emeritus, St. Paul Synod, ELCA

Written with a sense of urgency and replete with practical suggestions, Beyond Guilt *is well designed for small group discussion.*

Ruth and Loren Halvorson, Founders of ARC Ecumenical Retreat Center

George Johnson confronts us in our comfortable compassion with honest questions. He forces us to wrestle with biblical texts and encourages us to live in solidarity with hungry and oppressed people.

Russ Melby, Iowa Regional Director, Church World Service/CROP

This book is a WOW! If only part of these issues were addressed, it would knock the socks off the Christian church, and bring about an authentic renewal.

Ruth Morris, Retired Teacher and Presbyterian Stephens Minister

Beyond Guilt convincingly calls Christians to move beyond inertia and inactivity, to embrace a new sense of passion concerning suffering and inequity in our world.

Betty Voskuil, Coordinator: Reformed Church World Service and Diaconal Ministries

This is a powerful book, nicely done, not too long, a good study book.

David Garber, Senior Book Editor, Herald Press (Mennonite Publishing House)

Johnson enlarges the picture of lively faith as he takes us from charity to justice and from priest to priesthood. An excellent resource. We plan to carry it.

Marjory Bankson, President, Faith at Work

Where do you send someone who is frustrated after confronting the realities of social and economic injustice? For Ministry of Money it has often been George Johnson's book. We are delighted it is available in its expanded form.

Robert Hadley, Ministry of Money, Related to Church of our Savior, Washington, DC

George Johnson shares with us his heartfelt topics stitched together into a quilt of discipleship. I want to use this in my church.

Mavis Anderson, Director: International Travel Seminars Center for Global Education, Augsburg College, MN

This book not only deserves to be reprinted. We need it. Please, please make it available to the folk we talk with on our Trips of Perspective. It's a great book.

Dale Stitt and Esther Armstrong, Journey into Freedom, Portland, OR

Hola! How refreshing to read the new chapters that have been aded to this book. From Priest to Priesthood is where the church needs to ask for forgiveness and repent.

Tony Machado, Todos Los Santos Lutheran Church, Minneapolis, MN

I found the book to be a very useful tool indeed, and welcome the new edition. The structure and chapter themes are well developed.

Don Christensen, CCIDD, Cuernavaca, Mexico

Commitment to justice, a just world order, and the rights of the poor jump out at you from every page of this wonderful little book. Pastor Johnson pastorally moves us out of guilt and "charity fatigue" towards a new commitment to justice. Good for students too.

Charles Amjad Ali, Martin Luther King Professor of Justice and Christian Community at Luther Seminary in MN and Former Director of Christian Study Centre, Rawalpindi, Pakistan

George S. Johnson takes us by the hand and leads us out of our bleak despair and cynicism about our troubled world to a place of brilliant hope. In Beyond Guilt, Johnson provides the tools and rich resources to sustain us on the journey.

George Regas, Rector Emeritus, All Saints Episcopal Church, Pasadena, CA

Beyond Guilt

Christian Response to Suffering

Expanded and Revised

George S. Johnson

Additional copies of this book are available for $7.95 each book + $2 S/H. (MN residents add 6.5% sales tax.) Special rates available for small groups. Send check or money order to:

George S. Johnson
% Adventure Publications
P.O.Box 269
Cambridge, MN 55008

Call 1-800-678-7006 for credit card orders.

BEYOND GUILT
Christian Response to Suffering
Revised and Expanded from *Beyond Guilt and Powerlessness*, Augsburg 1989

Scripture quotations unless otherwise noted are from The New Revised Standard Version of the *Bible*, copyright 1989 by Division of Christian Education, National Council of Churches. Used by permission.

Inside photo credits: Center for Global Education, Augsburg College
Cover design by Debb Soderman

ISBN 0-9703028-0-0

CONTENTS

DEDICATION AND GRATITUDE

To
VIVIAN ELAINE JOHNSON

A beautiful person whose gift of encouragement and commitment to our partnership in marriage has been an inspiration to me and many others.

In Memory of our son
TODD RUSSELL JOHNSON
1956-1971

And remembering with thanksgiving all the people whose lives were cut short because of their courage and willingness to go beyond guilt in their commitment to the poor and oppressed in the world.

WITH SPECIAL THANKS

To Robert Hadley, who persevered in his encouragement to reprint Beyond Guilt and Powerlessness.

To the 25 people who re-read the original version and gave me a green light to proceed in getting this expanded and revised version into circulation.

For the two small grants that helped make this book affordable.

To Stacy Pollard, Laurel Gray, Ruth Morris, Lowell Erdahl, Janet Nyquist, John Halvorson, Leigh Hanson, Angie Harris, Gerri Slabough and Debb Soderman for their help along the way.

To the many whose stories, quotes and insights are shared in this book.

PREFACE

If you are willing to dig and wrestle and sweat, this book by George S. Johnson is for you. If you are looking for literary comfort food and a relaxing read, then you may want to close this book and see about a refund.

The bottom lines of this energetic devotional book are these: God is a living God. The living God of Old and New Testaments loves this crazy, beautiful, suffering world – through the person of Jesus Christ – with an astoundingly gracious combination of mercy and justice. This living God cares specially for suffering and oppressed people. And this living God calls us into a lively discipleship that reflects God's mercy and justice within the context of today's troubled world.

The author thus creates a book of meditations in which we hear an amazing variety of voices – common folk and well-known leaders, international and homegrown, women and men, young and old. The author's own insights and stories and challenges join in with this chorus of many voices to move us from passive observation to active engagement.

Johnson thereby invites us to also join this earthly chorus. He invites us to dig deeply for the roots of present day hunger and injustice, to dig expectantly for the precious ore of patience, of courage, of speech, and to uncover and expose the false gods within our consumer society. He invites us to wrestle with the following (and not just the believing) of Jesus, with our unprecedented wealth and material resources, with the formidable gifts of ambiguity and complexity, with the doing of both charity (mercy) and justice. He invites us to sweat over hearing those harsh but salutary voices and over recognizing again our heavy burdens of silence and guilt and conformity. But even more, he invites us to sweat like long-distance runners, running a lifelong race of lively discipleship: singing and caring, discovering and connecting, and peacemaking.

A personal word. I know George. I know him rather well, actually. Over 20 years now. We've traveled together, we've worked together (he was my boss for four years!), we've done our weeping and our laughing. And we've done our share of wrestling and sweating with each other. Dear reader, please know that the author of this book loves the Lord and loves people. His many years of profoundly caring for God's people all over the world create a firm foundation for this book.

A final word. Lest we overestimate our meager efforts, please know that God is the One who in Christ digs so deeply to find us, to unearth us, to raise us up. God is the One who wrestles with us and our world to lift us and turn us towards life and light. God is the One who sweats over us and runs with us – giving everything God has to give, such Love, such Compassion, such Grace...for us, for all people.

John L. Halvorson
Evangelical Lutheran Church in America
World Hunger Program coordinator
July, 2000

INTRODUCTION

> *If I love you, I have to make you conscious of the things you don't see.*
>
> James Baldwin

This book is about hope – hope that energizes. Its purpose is to encourage people who want to move beyond feelings of guilt, powerlessness and fear in their response to the widespread and growing suffering and oppression of people and degradation of our environment. It is written with the conviction that God's people are called to believe that things can be different, and that with God we are not powerless. God is not powerless.

There is a growing sense of frustration and apathy toward long-range social responsibility. During my 25 years of involvement with the issues of hunger and poverty (seven as director of the hunger program of the former American Lutheran Church), I have come into contact with scores of people who wanted to respond, who wanted to act compassionately toward human suffering, but who felt trapped, confused and helpless.

Many life-threatening forces call for our attention these days. The wake up alarm is sounding. Some wonder if it is too late. Daniel Maguire has said it well: "If current trends continue, we will not." Our society, our world is in trouble. Homelessness, hunger, poverty, violence, war, racism, environmental crisis, greed, domination, sustainable agriculture, global health emergencies and corruption in high places are a few of the issues that confront us. Everything seems to be interconnected. Many have become involved and active but later have become discouraged or have lost their sense of urgency. Some have sympathized but turned their energies toward something easier to handle. A few have become upset and cynical out of frustration at not being able to make a difference or see any progress. Others have felt personally attacked or criticized for approaches that were being used, their patriotism questioned, their way of reading the *Bible* challenged.

GUILT, POWERLESSNESS AND FEAR

The most common causes of this sense of being trapped seem to be guilt, powerlessness and fear. These are three dragons that paralyze the church in its efforts to move beyond a surface kind of charity toward oppressed people. Today the church needs to be liberated from its apathy and fear. We need a fresh outpouring of the Holy Spirit who empowers people with hope.

Guilt is ours. We do things that cause disharmony in God's created order. Guilt doesn't cause. We do. Guilt happens because of failure to love our neighbor and because of our apathy toward creative responses to human suffering. We handle our guilt in many ways, sometimes destructively. People who care want to find ways to move beyond guilt, not avoid or deny it.

To avoid feeling guilty about a hungry world, we may stay at surface-level analysis or move to issues that are easier to solve. Or, as one chapter suggests, guilt may be preferred to making changes or facing the pain and uncertainty of solidarity with those who cry for justice. Could it be that while we complain about guilt, we actually prefer it to enlightened analysis and action? Has the church made it easier to find relief from guilt than to act responsibly in a suffering world?

Powerlessness is another dimension to the feeling of frustration. The issues are so complex. Analyses differ. We ask ourselves: "What can I do that will make a significant difference? Whom shall I believe? I've done the letter writing. I've gone to hunger conferences and workshops. I've tried to simplify my lifestyle. I give generously to hunger causes. I'm tired. Confused. How can I feel better about myself? My energy and motivation are drying up. I need to concentrate on positive things. Given the resulting frustration, why bother?" Such confusion often leads to paralysis and cynicism. A sense of defeat and despair plagues the human spirit when it is unable to move beyond powerlessness.

Fear is another hindrance to creative response to human suffering. The statistics are frightening. The future looks grim for all of us if things don't change. To get involved may lead to changes we're not ready to make. Beliefs and values may be challenged. Systems that have blessed us may be examined and found wanting. Our security and prosperity may be jeopardized. We can sleep better at night when ignorant of the reality of human suffering and its connection to our acceptable lifestyles. Who wants to be labeled radical or subversive? Because of these types of fears, we keep our distance from the tough questions. We escape into other worthy causes or none at all. Or we may gravitate toward a theology or church that emphasizes safer or other-worldly issues. A new reading of the *Bible* may upset our comfortable ideas about what God's will is and what the kingdom of heaven is really about.

As missionary Tom Soeldner put it, "We are all infected by fear that robs us of our humanity and then makes us a cause of fear to others. It is both a fear of things beyond our control and a fear related to our guilt for not doing those godly things that are within our power."

While I have encountered many people who felt trapped by guilt, powerlessness and fear, I also have had the privilege of knowing many others who, for one reason or another, were able to move beyond these frustrations and continue steadfast in the struggle. These people are an inspiration to all of us. Knowing that their experiences could be an encouragement to others, I have asked permission to include some of their stories, insights and discoveries in this resource. Though you may not recognize their names, they are people like all of us who are in the struggle and have not given up. Being surrounded by this cloud of witnesses can give us encouragement and perseverance to run with patience the race set before us.

STAGES IN THE JOURNEY

We are at different stages in our journey of faith and social responsibility. The journey is not always straight or forward. Sometimes we go back and forth or up and down. Progress may not always be measurable or visible. This should not discourage us. The apostle Paul reminds us that "now we see in a mirror dimly...now we know in part." The important thing is not to give up or accept easy escape routes. Again Paul's words encourage us, "Let us not grow weary in well-doing, for in due season we shall reap, if we do not lose heart." (Galatians 6:9)

The chapter titles do not mean to suggest that everyone moves from one particular experience to the other if they are responsible Christians. It may be that you will move back and forth, for example, from certainty to ambiguity and from ambiguity to certainty (see Chapter 16). You may not identify with some of the stories or struggles suggested in these chapters. Pick and choose what to read, depending on the place in which you find yourself at a given time. Be ready to come back another time. It's okay to wrestle with someone's approach or have a different experience. Be patient, open and ready to be influenced or nudged by the Spirit. God accepts you where you are but never wants to leave you the same.

AWAKEN, ENCOURAGE AND CHALLENGE

This book is meant to be a resource for reflection, encouragement, challenge and action. It can be used as a guide for small groups, adult education classes, servant ministry camps, a follow-up reading after a trip or encounter with people living in poverty or oppression, as a training tool for those called to lead or teach, or as a place to return for hope when discouragement sets in and darkness engulfs. The energy and hope you receive may come from someone else's experience or from an unexpected spin-off. The stories, quotations, verses, prayers, questions and pieces of art are intended to awaken thought, spark imagination and precipitate action. Reflection/Action suggestions are given for you to use, adapt or ignore as you may choose. The chapters are not arranged in any permanent order or design. Certainly they do not exhaust the list of experiences we have as we move beyond guilt and powerlessness.

You may recognize yourself in many of these stories. You will meet the Word in the words and be apprehended, exposed, summoned and empowered. It is good to wrestle with God and not let go until you are blessed, knowing that God won't let go of you. Sometimes the encounter with God raises questions more than it answers our questions. We often are taken by surprise, asked to accept paradox, or caught up in mystery. Remember the Spirit is like the wind. John's gospel says, "It blows where it wills and you know not from whence it comes or where it goes." You may not be able to explain what's happening to you. We all go through various conversions.

As you read you are invited to allow your imagination to carry your thoughts beyond the words on the page into the personal arena of your experiences and conversations with God. Take time to reflect on the questions raised for you. Allow feelings to surface. Learn to ponder. Feel free to pick up this resource for short periods of devotion or reflection. Share the experience you are having with others. Add your story to these as you move beyond the comfort zone, the stalemate or valley you may be in. May God bless your creative imagination and give you courage to act on behalf of others.

George S. Johnson
San Marcos, California
Severinelaine@aol.com

INTRODUCTION

> ## 2 CORINTHIANS 4 : 7 - 10, 16
>
> *But we have this treasure in earthen vessels, to show that the transcendent power belongs to God and not to us. We are afflicted in every way, but not crushed; perplexed, but not driven to despair; persecuted, but not forsaken; struck down, but not destroyed; always carrying in the body the death of Jesus, so that the life of Jesus may also be manifested in our bodies...So we do not lose heart.*

REFLECTION • ACTION

1. How would you describe the stage of your faith journey at this time as it relates to responding to human suffering and oppression? Where is your growing edge?

2. Who/what has inspired you to move beyond guilt, powerlessness and fear? How have they done this? Tell him/her and thank them.

3. What questions or frustrations might be helpful to share with others? What might be the next step for you to take in moving beyond where you are?

4. Form a small group to meet regularly around the theme of this book. Pool your resources of the books recommended. Check your library or Pastor's study. Collect articles from the newspaper that relate.

DISCIPLESHIP AND CELEBRATION

WHAT EMOTIONS DO YOU SEE?

FROM STRUGGLE TO CELEBRATION

It is a matter of doing justice, of standing up to be counted, a stand infused by the passion of the Holy Spirit; informed by wise perception of the wholeness, the breadth, the interdependence of the issues at hand; and empowered by prayer. Without prayer, passion may become restless, manic activity. Without prayer, wisdom is empty and becomes mere intellectualizing, the spinning of conceptual wheels to no particular end. Without prayer, for example, theology may be about God, but seldom draws us farther into God. Without prayer, justice is doomed to disillusionment because we are unable to see beyond what they can see and all we see is injustice.

Carter Heyward, Episcopal Priest

People who have not learned to celebrate in the midst of struggle soon burn out or become cynical and negative. Sometimes they quit and find a new cause to join. Without times of singing and celebration in our lives, we are no longer fun to live with; we end up alienating people rather than drawing them into our circle of friends and supporters. Whenever I have given a workshop or seminar on hunger and poverty I include music. As Walter Wink says, "Singing about is a way of bringing about."

Those who constantly struggle to survive in the midst of poverty and oppressive situations find ways to celebrate. Music, dance and humor are often used to lift their spirits and give cause to enjoy one another. They demonstrate that God has made us to celebrate. They become energized with hope by taking time to celebrate.

We celebrate God's presence and the gift of shared bread when we gather for the Eucharist. We celebrate creation when we take time to enjoy flowers, birds and our bodies. We celebrate each other when we take time to be with one another without a business agenda. We celebrate the earth when we eat and enjoy food. We celebrate the image of God within us with healthy humor, creative art forms, a sense of accomplishment and human touch.

Our efforts to alleviate human suffering will always be a struggle. There will be pain and disappointment. The gift of celebration will keep us from despair and distortion. It will send us back into the struggle with renewed vision and hope. Setting aside times to celebrate and pray is an investment in hope.

Christians have set a high priority on gathering together regularly for worship. The center of focus is the good news, the gospel. Worship time is celebration time. We need worship forms that release power both within the individual and in the community. In the setting of corporate worship we can lift up the cries of pain as well as the reasons to rejoice, knowing that we are all one body in Christ. In our liturgies and prayers we weep with those who weep and rejoice with those who rejoice.

God's people have learned to celebrate even in the midst of darkness and chaos. In darkness there is often the birthing of something new. Creativity comes from the depths, says Matthew Fox, and part of the depths is our darkness, chaos and uncertainty. The chaos of Good Friday yielded to the creativity and newness of Easter. Knowing this, we are encouraged to celebrate in the midst of struggle. I like the way Jim Wallis phrased the dedication of his new book *Faith Works*: "To my wife Joy Carroll Wallis, who turns the walk of faith into a dance of life."

OTHER VOICES

If We Could Not Laugh, We Could Not Survive

Yesterday I joined in celebrating the retirement of Dr. Wolfram Kistner from the South African Council of Churches. He is a small, fragile man of immense courage and perseverance, dedicated both to the gospel of Jesus Christ and to the liberation struggle in southern Africa. It was the day after the South African government's latest crackdown on the most effective groups and individuals involved in that struggle. Frank Chikane, the general secretary of the council, was one of those persons who paid tribute to Dr. Kistner.

Frank noted the contrast between such a celebration and the devastating context of the government's action of the previous day. It reminded him, he said, of his time in detention, when he was given food so rotten he could not eat it and told to wash his dishes and himself with the water from the only source in his cell, the toilet. He said that when the prisoners had any time together, they would share such stories and laugh at them, sometimes uncontrollably. Or when they spoke about certain aspects of their torture at the hands of the police, they could laugh at such horrible things, and he told them, "If we could not laugh, we could not survive."

I think that perhaps this laughter is what remains of faith when one has known only the cross and death. People stand amid the groaning of all creation, as if before Easter: open to its inbreaking, longing for it, but not assuming that they know either its time or its character. They stand in the community of victims and witnesses, waiting for – what?–waiting for the kingdom of God. What else could there possibly be to answer the victims' anguished impotence? Could it be that this laughter is a mustard seed's worth of faith? Could it be that it is the kingdom already breaking in?

Tom Soeldner, missionary in South Africa

Justice, The Function of Worship

The primary setting in which Israel experienced and celebrated justice was her worship. Worship in Israel was not a setting preoccupied with the other world, or with sacrifices only, which is a distorted picture. No, justice and the advancement of justice and the proclamation of justice was the very function of worship, to mediate God's justice for the world. Worship in Israel, whether it was influenced by the Exodus-Sinai tradition or the David Temple tradition of Jerusalem, had in its center the experience of the gift of God's justice and the proclamation of justice for the world and for Israel. The Psalms document these facts clearly. So do the traditions of the Exodus-Sinai covenant in the Pentateuch and elsewhere, and even the priestly code expresses, through its structure of Leviticus, that worship and social ethos belong together.

Rolf Knierim, Old Testament Professor

I want the parishes in my diocese to be as well prepared, equipped and organized to serve the poor in their community as they are to celebrate the Eucharist.

William Frey, Episcopal Bishop

EXODUS 24:11
They beheld God, and ate and drank.

ISAIAH 58:6-9
Is not this the fast that I choose: to loose the bonds of wickedness, to undo the thongs of the yoke, to let the oppressed go free, and to break every yoke? Is it not to share your bread with the hungry, and bring the homeless poor into your house; when you see the naked, to cover him, and not to hide yourself from your own flesh? Then shall your light break forth like the dawn, and your healing shall spring up speedily; your righteousness shall go before you, the glory of the Lord shall be your rear guard. Then you shall call, and the Lord will answer; you shall cry, and he will say, 'Here I am.'

REFLECTION • ACTION

1. What is it about music that lifts our spirits and binds us together? What did Martin Luther mean when he said, "whoever sings prays twice?" Sing or hum a familiar tune throughout the day.

2. Celebration is meant to be done in community. It is often accompanied by eating together. What does this tell us about celebration? Recall the times when Jesus ate with others. Remember with thanksgiving a special meal of celebration in your life.

3. Think of the different things (meanings, ideas, events) we celebrate at the Eucharist. How does it empower us for the struggle? How can we keep the Lord's Supper from becoming too individualistic, institutional, exclusive or ritualistic?

4. Read *Proclaim Jubilee* a Spirituality for the Twenty-First Century by Maria Harris, Westminster John Knox Press, 1996; and/or *The Eucharist and Human Liberation* by Tissa Balasuriya, Orbis, 1977 and/or *To Celebrate* from Alternatives.

FROM BELIEVING TO FOLLOWING

> *I don't know who – or what – put the question; I don't know when it was put. I don't even remember answering. But at some moment I did answer yes to someone – or something – and from that hour I was certain that existence is meaningful and that, therefore, my life, in self-surrender, had a goal. From that moment I have known what it means "not to look back," and "to take no thought for the morrow."*
>
> Dag Hammarskjöld
> UN General Secretary

When new members are received into our churches, we seldom ask them if they have responded to the call to follow Jesus Christ. We ask them about their beliefs. "Do you believe in Jesus?" No new member has questioned me as to what it means to believe. Most find it easy to say they believe in God and in Jesus. As Bonhoeffer says, "we haven't asked any awkward questions."

In the Sunday morning service some stand and recite a Confession of Faith. "We believe in God the Father Almighty...in Jesus Christ...in the Holy Spirit." Would it make a difference if we stood and said, "I am a follower of Jesus, who was executed because of his subversive love for me and for my neighbor" or, "I have decided to follow Jesus this coming week in all I say, do, or think"?

Could it be that in our desire to keep the gospel pure, and be clear on salvation as a gift, we have failed to extend the call to follow Jesus Christ as it is given in the Scriptures? Have we been too afraid of the role of decision on our part? Isn't coming to a decision a work of the Spirit also?

Jim Wallis, in his book *Call to Conversion,* says that neither evangelicals nor liberals have grasped the meaning of conversion for these times. It is his contention that any conversion (repentance and faith) that is removed from social and political reality is simply not biblical. His book lays out a strong argument for the recovery of an emphasis on conversion in the church in order for the church to be able to respond to a suffering world.

Such a conversion emphasis necessitates believing and following Jesus. Many people who have moved beyond the trap of guilt and powerlessness talk about their conversion, sometimes their second or third conversion. By this they mean a turnaround in their lives, seeing things from a new perspective. Such conversions do not negate our baptismal covenant but rather awaken us to what Martin Luther calls the daily death and resurrection meaning of our baptism. Every day we answer the call to believe and follow. Dorothy Soelle reminds us that in saying yes to Jesus there is a decisive no also involved; for example, a no to the royal empires of today that call for our primary allegiance.

In the prologue to his book *Jesus – A Revolutionary Biography*, John Dominic Crossan reminds the reader that there is more to being a follower of Jesus than facts and beliefs. He gives an imaginary dialogue with the historical Jesus who says, "I read your book, Dominic, and it's quite good. So now are you ready to live by my vision and join me in my program?" "I don't think I have the courage, Jesus, but I did describe it quite well didn't I, and the method was especially good, wasn't it?" "Thank you Dominic, for not falsifying the message to suit your own incapacity. That at least is something." "Is it enough, Jesus?" "No, Dominic, it is not."

OTHER VOICES

Are You Following Jesus or Believing in Christ?

It began innocently enough – a friend recommending a book, *Christology at the Crossroads* by Jon Sobrino. The Salvadoran Jesuit blew most of my theological ducks out of the water. He threw a hat down on my Scrabble board and messed up many of my combinations. He forced me to contend for the ground I had claimed. The question that Jon Sobrino put to me I must share with you: Are you following Jesus, or believing in Christ?

Plunge into the Gospels anywhere and you will likely find Jesus asking someone to follow. The verb is *akaloutheo*. It represents a dominant motif. Why, then, do we hear so little about following Jesus in the church today? I've been in, with, and around the church for more than 50 years, and no one has ever asked me, "Are you following Jesus?" Not when I was in the communicants' class; not when I joined the church; not when I became a candidate for the ministry; not when I was ordained; and never in any of my services of installation. Always the questions have dealt with belief: Do you believe in God – Father, Son and Spirit? Do you believe in the veracity of the Scriptures and the Westminster Confession? Do you believe in the unity and purity of the church?

It is as though we held the notion that following Jesus was "in" until the crucifixion and went out with the resurrection – that we can take up with Jesus on easier terms on the other side of Easter.

Do you believe in Christ? It isn't so hard to answer that. What is wanted is an affirmative response to treasured propositions about the second person of the Trinity. But when someone asks, "Are you following Jesus?" this can get to be expensive. This question has to do with my life-style, my attitudes, my values, my surrender.

If I'm following Jesus, why am I such a good insurance risk? If I'm following Jesus, why, when I have done my giving, have I so much left over for myself? If I'm following Jesus, why do my closets bulge when so many are unclothed? If I'm following Jesus, why do I have so many friends among the affluent and so few among the poor? If I'm following Jesus, why do I have so much privacy in a world that is starved for love? If I'm following Jesus, why am I tempted to overeat in a world where so many beg for bread? If I'm following Jesus, why am I getting on so well in a world that marked him out for death?

Are you following Jesus or believing in Christ? Unfair you say: The two are inseparable. Theoretically, yes, but pragmatically, no. We separate them all the time. If we must err, let us err on the side of following. *For one can believe without following, but one cannot follow without believing.*

Ernest Campbell, Riverside Church, New York City

From: *Cost of Discipleship*

We have gathered like eagles round the carcass of cheap grace, and there we have drunk of the poison that has killed the life of following Christ.. We have given away the Word and sacraments wholesale; we baptized, confirmed and absolved a whole nation without asking awkward questions or insisting on strict conditions. Our humanitarian sentiment made us give that which was holy to the scornful and unbelieving. We poured forth unending streams of grace. But the call to follow Jesus was hardly ever heard.

Dietrich Bonhoeffer

Spiritual Renewal that Empowers

Please don't think I'm a real "fundie." That's not my background at all. For the past 10 or 15 years I've been working to inform, inform, inform and motivate, motivate, motivate and I've come to the conclusion that all the information and motivation goes just so far. My husband and I are in the midst of a very radical change in our ministry and lifestyle. We feel joyful and thankful and pray that we are being more faithful to our Lord. This is only possible because of a spiritual renewal in our lives that is empowering us to change. I feel so strongly that the whole world needs to change, especially the United States. Our external world will never change unless/until our internal/spiritual selves are renewed. That's the starting point.

Deborah Peters, Montana Hunger Advocate

> Matthew 16:24-25
>
> *Then Jesus told his disciples, "If any man would come after me, let him deny himself and take up his cross and follow me. For whoever would save his life will lose it, and whoever loses his life for my sake will find it."*

REFLECTION • ACTION

1. Think through the Hammarskjold quote. Has there ever been a moment when you said yes? Have there been any mini- or maxi-conversions in your life? How did your perspective change?

2. Why is it easier to think about believing in Jesus than to think about following Jesus? How do you understand the difference? Discuss the Bonhoeffer quote.

3. Who has been influential in the formation of your Christian life? If there have been any important experiences or turning points, tell about them. The exercise of writing them out may also be helpful.

4. Read *Faith Works* by James Wallis, Random House, 2000; and/or *Subversive Spirituality* by Eugene H. Peterson, Eerdmans, 1997; and/or *Following Jesus* (small group study guide) by George S. Johnson, Augsburg, 1995.

FROM SILENCE TO SPEECH

> *In Germany in the 1930s they first came for the Communists and I didn't speak up because I wasn't a Communist. Then they came for the Jews, and I didn't speak up because I wasn't a Jew. Then they came for the trade unionists, and I didn't speak up. Then they came for the Catholics, and I didn't speak up because I was a Protestant. Then they came for me...and by that time no one was left to speak up.*
>
> Pastor Martin Niemoller

Walter Brueggemann, in his magazine article "Theological Education: Healing the Blind Beggar" (Christian Century, April 5-12, 1986), uses the story of blind Bartimaeus in Mark 10:46-52 to demonstrate what he feels theological education should be helping churches to do. He mentions four things: "Theological education that promises healing and liberation:

1. must have sociological imagination, which includes awareness of the world around us as well as the world Jesus lived in

2. must face the fact that a key issue in healing, salvation and liberation is power

3. must recognize that the first step in gaining power is bringing things to speech

4. must be unashamedly Christological, not hesitant to proclaim that Christ came to set at liberty the oppressed. He came to change the situation in people's lives and in the world."

The third point highlights the importance of speech when the blind beggar cries out "Son of David, have mercy on me." He knows it is Messiah time, says Brueggemann, the time when the blind see, the poor have their debts canceled, and beggars become citizens again (Luke 7:22-23).

Brueggemann goes on to say, "We face a crisis of speech in our time. History moves and life is transformed when the powerless get speech. We need therefore, in all our institutions, to be asking: Who has speech? Who does the talking? Who does the decisive speaking?"

Those who are concerned about human suffering are learning to speak out and give voice to the voiceless. It is important to resist the pressures to be silent. The turning point in the Mark narrative is when the blind beggar is able to speak of his pain. Transforming energy is released and hope is renewed when our silence is broken and when the "little" ones are able to cry out. We move beyond powerlessness when we use our gifts and resources and our voices to enable victims to be heard.

OTHER VOICES

We Haven't the Right to Keep Silent

A chilling account comes to me from Bangkok: A friend tells me of the fate of the Cambodian refugees whom we had visited shortly before this spring. They are now being moved from camp to camp; everyone wants them out of the way. This human burden is more than we can bear. If only these people would just disappear so that we could sleep in peace again!

In the meantime, hunger continues to ravage the emaciated bodies of starving children, while poverty and wretchedness darken their horizon.

Last February I asked myself the question, Can an entire people die? Now I would formulate it differently: Will we stand by and let them die? We spend billions of dollars on nuclear arms and billions more on cosmetics; we kneel before the sacred shrine of all-holy oil and make fine-sounding speeches for the entertainment and delectation of the peanut gallery in the United Nations. We sink into hypocrisy and indifference. And all the while, in the poor nations, the shadow of poverty lengthens from day to day. And the shadow of fear as well.

I would never have imagined that I should one day feel compelled to vent my rage against the present as I have against the past.

From Paris, a series of images: Starving men and women somewhere in Uganda. Bodies so emaciated that they are almost transparent. Shriveled children expiring in their turn only a few hours later. "You have to shout; you have to raise a cry of outrage," says my friend who sent me the documents.

And so I shout. I bellow. I alert my journalist comrades. I call up senators and high-level functionaries: We haven't the right to keep silent! An entire people is stepping down into darkness before our very eyes; if we do nothing to save them, we shall have been accomplices in their deaths!

But – and I am ashamed to say it – people are tired. Tired of fighting for yet another cause. Tired of throwing themselves into yet another struggle. Biafra, Bangladesh, the Congo, Cambodia and now Uganda: There is a limit to human comprehension! A time comes when people avert their eyes out of an instinct for self-preservation.

Nevertheless, we have no choice. Indifference is a crime. Not to choose is in itself a choice, as Camus said. To do nothing is to let death do everything.

As for myself, I have seen too much in my life to stand by and watch. It may not be in our power to evade our own suffering, but it is within our power to give our suffering some meaning. And it is in combating the suffering of others that we find meaning in our own.

Elie Wiesel,
Holocaust survivor

Politics determines the kind of world you will be born in; ~ the kind of education, health care and job you eventually get; how you will spend your old age and even how you die. The church must address itself to, and be involved in, anything that affects life as greatly as this.

Rev. Walter S. Taylor

> ### EXODUS 2:23-25
>
> *In the course of those many days the king of Egypt died. And the people of Israel groaned under their bondage, and cried out for help, and their cry under bondage came up to God. And God heard their groaning, and God remembered his covenant with Abraham, with Isaac, and with Jacob. And God saw the people of Israel and God knew their condition.*

REFLECTION • ACTION

1. Think about who has speech, who does the talking in your community. How does your congregation or group give voice to the voiceless? Can this be encouraged through worship and liturgy in the church?

2. Choose one group of suffering people on whom to concentrate. Take time to listen and enter into their pain. Think of ways you can help break the silence of those on the margins of society.

3. Invite musicians, artists, writers and teachers to use their gifts to lift up the cry of those whose voices are not being heard. What gift can you use to this end?

4. Read *Walking with the Poor* by Bryant L. Myer, Orbis Books/World Vision, 1999; and/or *Jesus' Plan for a New World* (The Sermon on the Mount), by Richard Rohr, OFM, St. Anthony Messenger Press, 1996.

FROM PRIEST TO PRIESTHOOD

> We live in a generation where the unfinished business of the Reformation may at last be completed. Nearly five hundred years ago, Martin Luther, John Calvin and others unleashed a revolution that promised to liberate the church from a hierarchical structure by rediscovering the "priesthood" of all believers. But the Reformation never fully delivered on its promise. The Reformation started something with radical implications, but failed to follow through.
>
> Greg Ogden,
> The New Reformation

While Director of the Hunger Program for my denomination (1980-1987) I visited many parishes in the United States. In almost every congregation I found a remnant of people who were both aware of and concerned about the crisis of poverty, hunger and environmental degradation. Some of them were discouraged because their pastor was not supportive of their efforts. They were eager to alert the whole congregation about root causes and make social justice an important part of the church's mission, but their congregational leaders had other priorities or thought it too risky. Eugene Peterson in The Contemplative Pastor says too many pastors have stepped into the role of chaplains to the culture instead of subversives to the culture. Some Christians in exile have felt compelled to leave the church because it is too preoccupied maintaining structures or secondary issues. Churches can become so self serving and pre-occupied with church growth, purity rituals and religious ecstacy, that there is little energy left for ministry to the poor and oppressed.

In most congregations the pastor is the gatekeeper; the one who decides what gets attention in the church. Sad, but true. Ogden is right. The

Reformation did not make a complete break from a hierarchical conception of ministry. While Luther and Calvin both emphasized that all Christians are priests called to be ministers and functioning members of the body of Christ, they failed to lead the church to act on this important biblical teaching. Most Catholic and Protestant churches today continue to be clergy dominated. The pastors and priests are what Ogden calls dispensers of grace and guardians of church order. Social issues that need attention for the most part are controlled by the designated holy minister. Ernest Campbell says it well, "Most lay people see themselves as part of the support system for the clergy. But the reverse is the way it ought to be."

Thomas Cahill, author of *Desire of the Everlasting Hills* – the World Before and After Jesus – writes how Christianity was seriously compromised by being brought into the power structures of the Roman Empire (Edict of Tolerance 313). He argues, however, for three other developments that more severely weakened the Christian movement in its early history. They are: its alienation from Judaism, its division into two classes – clergy and lay, and its fragmentation into three feuding branches – Orthodox, Catholic and Protestant.

How many times have you heard someone say to a promising candidate for the seminary, "Have you considered the ministry…" or "You'd make a good minister." Yet ministry is not something that is performed by one designated person in each parish. Every Christian is called to be a minister. Our use of the term ministry lends itself to a class distinction between those ordained and those not. Ogden talks boldly about the institutional entrapment of the church. He says we are captive to a structure that encourages the idea that the ordained are special ministers who have the responsibility to dispense grace through the word and sacraments. This suggests that not all Christians are ordained to ministry. Such thinking has greatly weakened our effectiveness in the world. One area where this is visibly evident is the church's call to work for justice in the world.

Of course leadership and structure is necessary when you have numbers of diverse people working and worshipping together. Pastoral leadership is important in the biblical models of a covenant people seeking to follow Jesus in a turbulent world. The paradigm shift toward less hierarchical structure and more involvement of laity does not eliminate the need for leadership and pastors. What it does is give the ministry back to the people. The church needs to move from priest or minister domination to the priesthood of all believers where every member is called, responsible and accountable. We need to be more aware of subtle trends that support the institutional entrapment of the church.

One of the hopeful signs of renewal toward the priesthood of all believers is the small group movement taking hold in many churches. Robert Wuthnow, Princeton University professor and sociologist of religion, in *Sharing the Journey* calls it a quiet revolution taking place in our society. People are not satisfied, he says, with one person telling them what to believe. They want to think about the church's proclamation, and discuss it. There is a growing desire to find support from the Christian community, a kind of support not experienced from an hour in the pew every Sunday. Arthur Baranowski in *Creating Small Faith Communities* calls the leaders of small groups "pastoral facilitators." This is an interesting shift in the Roman Catholic use of the term pastor. Laity can become ministers to one another. They can do pastoral ministry.

What does all this have to do with moving beyond guilt? It means that there is a need for all of us to address the social justice issues in our society. We dare not wait till the clergy give us permission. It means that if the church is to make a difference in the world we need to revisit the Reformation teaching of the priesthood of all believers. The church must find ways to be free from the tradition that gives ministry over to the ordained few. It means passing power to the people of God who are moved by the suffering of people and want to work together to respond with compassion. It means letting people who have left the church because it has been too clergy or institution focused, know that things can change, and invite them to join us in our struggle.

OTHER VOICES

The Church of the Future

In the fourth century at the Council of Nicaea, lay people were pushed to the edges, and clergy, especially the bishops, took over the Christian movement. It has continued thus until today. To be a lay person after Nicaea was "a concession to human frailty." They were second class citizens in the kingdom of God. The church of the future must be primarily a lay church, with the laity as participants playing the game, and with clergy on the sidelines as the coaches of a team, as the guides of an essentially lay movement.

E. Stanley Jones

There is an old Negro Spiritual that says, "Has you got good religion?"...Bad religion stays in the church. Good religion breaks loose in the world. Bad religion hangs around the altar. Good religion goes down Jerico road.

Rev. Dr. Charles Adams

In our time it may well be that the greatest single bottleneck to the renewal and outreach of the church is the division of roles between clergy and laity that results in a hesitancy to trust the laity with significant responsibility, and in turn a reluctance on the part of laity to trust themselves as authentic ministers of Christ, either in the church or outside the church.

Robert Munger, Fuller Seminary

1 PETER 2:9

But you are a chosen race, a royal priesthood, a holy nation, God's own people, in order that you proclaim the mighty acts of him who called you out of darkness into his marvelous light.

REFLECTION • ACTION

1. What are some signs for you that suggest our churches are too pastor focused and fail to put into practice the Reformation principle of the priesthood of all believers? Discuss the E. Stanley Jones quote.

2. Think of someone who has been a pastor/priest to you who has not been an ordained minister. How did they minister to you?

3. What needs to happen in order for the church to be more focused on training disciples than on church maintenance and institutional structure? Discuss the value of small groups for the 21st century church.

4. Which is more important in your church: understanding Christian teachings or discovering and renewing relationships? What are priorities in church life today? How are they demonstrated?

5. Read *The New Reformation* by Greg Ogden, Zondervan, 1990; *The Unnecessary Pastor*, Marva Dawn and Eugene Peterson, Eerdmans, 2000; and/or *Creating Small Faith Communities* by Arthur Baranowski, Bethany Press, 1988.

FROM URGENCY TO PATIENCE

> *Politics is the art of making possible tomorrow what seems impossible today.*
>
> Edvard Hambro

Most North Americans are in a hurry to get things done. When something needs fixing we are programmed to find the solution and get on with living. When we experience a pain, we usually can take a pill and be done with it. It is not easy for us to live with pain, unanswered questions and problems that are not solved by our technology, wealth, or military might.

When you add to this the urge to see results, the desire for a sense of accomplishment and progress, you begin to realize why patience is needed when you give yourself to the cause of justice and peace in the world. As one of my friends said, "Put on your walking shoes because it's going to be a long journey and the terrain is often uphill."

Moses and the Israelites were in the wilderness 40 years before they reached the promised land. It must have seemed like a long time. Jesus was 40 days and 40 nights in the desert following his baptism and commissioning by John the Baptist. Missionary A. E. Gunderson went to West Africa in the early part of this century, in obedience to Matthew 28:19: "Go...make disciples of all nations." It was 12 years before he had his first baptism. The story of the saints is a story of patience and perseverance.

We must be careful, however, to make a distinction between patience and indifference. Many reports of human suffering are emergency situations. It might be a crisis of life or death for the people involved. They cry for help now. Each day that goes by means more and more death and destruction. Urgent action is needed. Our delay tactics, procrastination and apathy are not what is meant by patience. Some of us need to be shaken out of our sleep because the situation is urgent. There are things we can begin doing today that will make a difference.

For all who would move beyond guilt and powerlessness there needs to be a balance of urgency and patience. We need to act and we need to wait. There is a time for retreat and reflection and a time for picking up the towel and basin for washing feet. We may not see the justice we are working for come about in our lifetime but this will not discourage us. The vision and the promise are enough.

OTHER VOICES

A Palestinian Talks About Waiting

When I look at Jewish history in the decades before 1950, I have the impression that the Jews underwent such a pressure of persecution, of oppression and the worst was the concentration camps. The concentration camps were a result of the real oppression. Once they were stereotyped as just dirty Jews – *Schmutziger Jude*. Who likes to have schmutz (dirt) at home, or in his streets, or in his towns? Everybody would like to get rid of the dirt. And that's what happened in Europe. They wanted to get rid of the dirt and when they opened the concentration camps, we saw that what was there was not dirt but children of God, massacred and slaughtered. Only then did the Western world begin to understand that the real dirt was not on the face of the Jew, rather, it was in the mind of Hitler and those who supported his criminal philosophy. I must come to rest with that because one day, because of these massacres of the Jews, I heard my father telling us in upper Galilee in our village, "Children, within a few days, we will receive Jewish soldiers in our village. They might have machine guns but they do not kill. They are just like us – persecuted people. Poor fellows who were lucky enough to escape a devil called Hitler trying to alienate them. And as persecuted brothers, we have to receive them and I ask you to give them your beds to sleep, and we will prepare for them food and accommodation."

Those times I remember very well because we were asked to sleep on the roof of our house. In Galilee you can do it. You can sleep on the roof of your house and you can count the stars in heaven. It's so beautiful. Therefore we were happy that the soldiers came, and we were sleeping in the open. The soldiers came. We received them. We remained together with our new brothers for more than 10 days, after which we were asked very politely, very peacefully, to leave the village for two weeks because of what will become the golden call: "security reasons." They gave us a written promise that within two weeks we shall return to our homes. Therefore we took nothing at all. We even gave the keys to the Jewish officer. We went and lived for two weeks in grottos and under trees in the open, waiting that these two weeks be finished.

They did not come to an end and here we are with 40 years of deportation, of deprivation, waiting for the two weeks to end. When we got really despaired of implementing the promise of those whom we considered being our brothers, we were prevented from any kind of violence because our elderly people, like my father, used to continually tell us and he still tells us today: "You have been driven out from your homes with utter violence and extreme trickery. You have to remember your task to return but never use the same methods because the one who used violence once, violence will be used against him. And with violence you can produce something which is called more violence and what we need to solve our problem is rather to conquer not the land of others but the hearts of those frightened people who consider themselves to be our enemies."

This is very important to understand, how we Jews and Palestinians came to that murderous conflict. After two weeks, my father and the elderly people tried to come back to their village. They were forbidden the right to return. They waited one year, two years. They went to the Supreme Court of Justice in Jerusalem. The decision was in their favor but nowadays, as you know in your society and everywhere in any human society, right alone is a dead letter. Right alone can leave you to be crucified and killed and when you are killed as a righteous person, you are a criminal. You are a dirty person, nasty. Maybe in the so-called free world you become a Communist. If you are from those people who lose their village, their country, their homeland, and you try to say, "I want it back," you are only right, and you are killed. They call you only terrorists while the others are freedom fighters. It's very sad. Very sad. So we had only the right, we did not have the might, and now as an adult, I thank God a million times that we did not have the might and had the right only. Because might corrupts very much, and with the might you can wrong the right and right the wrong. And that's what happened to us. Although we were frightened. Although we accepted to share everything with our brothers. Since we were the mightiless side, we were portrayed as simple refugees. Nothing else. Nobody asked why are these people refugees? What have they done to be refugees? Therefore compassionate, good Christians sent money to help these poor refugees survive.

Now I know that money is a very harmful help to give to your brother. Money is very often a kind of conscience tranquilizer. You know what it's like?

Sometimes like many of our Christian prayers. If you feel sympathy or you are moved by the story, the experience of any of your brothers, you hasten to tell him, "I will pray for you." I wish these prayers would be stopped. I wish nobody would pray for me or for the Jew because he is moved by our plight and tragedy, and if anybody wants to pray, it's time that he pray for himself to be converted, to make enough space in his heart and his life for one Jew and for one Palestinian. The charity prayer is not a Christian prayer. And the money "conscience tranquilizer" is no help given to God.

Father Elias Chacour

One Step at a Time

One of the greatest evils of the day among those outside of prison is their sense of futility. Young people say what good can one person do? What is the sense of our small effort? They cannot see that we must lay one brick at a time, take one step at a time. We can be responsible only for the one action of the present moment. But we can beg for an increase of love in our hearts that will vitalize and transform all our individual actions and know that God will take them and multiply them, as Jesus multiplied the loaves and fishes.

Dorothy Day, Catholic Worker

HEBREWS 12: 1-2

Therefore, since we are surrounded by so great a crowd of witnesses, let us also lay aside every weight, and sin which clings so closely, and let us run with perseverance the race that is set before us, looking to Jesus the pioneer and perfecter of our faith, who for the joy that was set before him endured the cross, despising the shame, and is seated at the right hand of the throne of God.

GALATIANS 6:9

So let us not grow weary in doing what is right for we will reap at harvest time if we do not give up.

REFLECTION • ACTION

1. Read Hebrews 11. What experiences have you had that have taught you patience? What is the difference between patience and apathy? Patience and perseverance?

2. Moses went back to Pharaoh ten times, asking him to let the Israelites go. What do you think sustained him? What memories of patience do you have from the lives of Martin Luther King, Jr., Oscar Romero, Nelson Mandela, Mahatma Ghandi, Caesar Chavez or Mother Teresa?

3. Get to know someone you feel has exercised great patience in addressing a wrong. Find out what has helped this person balance urgency and patience. This might be done through reading various biographies.

4. Read *Gracias* by Henri Nouwen, Harper & Row, 1983; and/or *I Am a Palestinian Christian* by Mitri Raheb, Fortress Press, 1995; and/or *Gustavo Guitierrez* by Robert McAfee Brown, Orbis, 1990.

FROM WEEPING TO SINGING

> *Only grief permits newness. If God had not grieved when hearing the mocking voice of nations there would have been no healing. If Jeremiah had not cried his way through Chapter 4 and Chapter 8, God would not have had a new word to speak in Chapters 30-31...The very structure of the gospel is an argument that pain felt and articulated in God's heart permits new possibilities in the historical process – the good news concerns God's transformed heart.*
>
> Walter Brueggemann

I was on sabbatical from my parish in Long Beach, California. At the School of Theology in Claremont, CA I was enrolled in a semester-long seminar called "World Hunger and Christian Institutional Response." In different ways we were exposed to the reality of needless suffering of people all over the world. One day in class I started to cry. It came out of nowhere. Tears formed in my eyes. I was embarrassed. To avoid being seen in tears, I lifted my textbook to cover my face. You aren't supposed to cry in class at the graduate level.

We all have heard stories or seen pictures of starvation and torture that are enough to make us weep. Even those of us who have been taught to hide our emotions surely find it difficult not to shed a tear or two when confronted with some of the hideous things that are happening today to innocent people and to God's handiwork in creation. Weeping is a human response to suffering, whether mine or someone else's.

It is important to allow ourselves to weep. Weeping and grieving are parts of the redemptive process, the healing process. Jesus wept. Why shouldn't we?

Theologian Walter Brueggemann says that the church has lost its capacity to grieve and thereby is unable to become a liberating force in society.

Perhaps our reluctance to look at the bloated bellies and haunting faces of starving children is a sign of this loss. It might be that in our haste to help, we don't sit long enough with those who suffer and weep with them. It was Ezekiel who sat by the river with the outcasts and wept. After that he was empowered to speak a prophetic word. Jesus wept over the city of Jerusalem, then made his way to the temple and on to Calvary.

When we wipe away our tears (not the same as avoiding them) we can be energized for action. We move through and from weeping to singing. Some of the weeping may continue in our songs, such as the laments in the Psalms. Singing is such an important part of our response to human suffering. Singing and music lift our spirits. Music is the language of the heart. Many times, when we don't know what to say or how to cope, a song best expresses our faith, our hope. Music moves us. It empowers us when nothing else can. Music touches our emotions.

It is important to find music and lyrics that fit the occasion. Sometimes an old hymn will do it. At other times we yearn for new songs and new liturgies that give us encouragement and hope. Songs from other cultures and nations are an inspiration. We seek words that address the experiences of pain as well as the assurances from God that God is indeed present in the struggle. We need to encourage people with the gift of music that can help us move beyond guilt and powerlessness.

OTHER VOICES

We Sing Mary's Song

Martin Luther sent a letter to Prince John Frederick, Duke of Saxony, introducing his commentary on the Magnificat (Luke 1:47-55). Luther said that it is a fine custom to sing the Magnificat at vespers each night. He commended the Magnificat to Prince John Frederick, saying that it "ought to be learned and kept in mind by all who would rule well and be helpful lords."

Each time we sing the Magnificat, we proclaim to each other what sort of God we believe in and especially, as Luther says, how God deals with those of low and high degree. Luther says we sing it for three reasons: (1) to strengthen our faith, (2) to comfort the lowly and (3) to terrify the mighty. We will look at these reasons in reverse order.

To terrify the mighty. As a group of theologians and church leaders, we fit more properly in the category of the mighty than in that of the lowly. Most of us are white, the color of privilege in our hemisphere. We are mostly middle-class, living very comfortable lives, and rich by most comparisons. Most of us are male, another privileged group in our hemisphere. As church leaders and teachers, we are often highly educated. We are the intellectually elite. We are employed in positions of respect and leadership.

Some of us fit all these categories of the mighty. All of us fit in most of them. Luther said, "The mightier you are, the more you must fear, when you sing the Magnificat. We fear because we sing in faith, believing God does bring down the mighty."

It is risky for the mighty to sing the Magnificat. It might mean moving from the center to the fringes. It might mean leaving theologically proper talk to engage in simple, frank discussions. Or it might mean risking tenured positions in our schools of theology or jobs in the church bureaucracy, as we speak clearly and forthrightly about the implications of our faith. It might mean risking our intellectual credibility as we respect the visions of poor Indians of Guadalupe.

But we take the risk! We sing the Magnificat in faith, knowing that fear can lead us to repentance, and repentance prepares us for the coming reign of God.

To comfort the lowly. We sing to proclaim comfort to the lowly. Each time we sing Mary's song, we are called to believe once again that God has deep regard for the lowly, the hungry, the poor, the little ones.

I was deeply moved by the story of the poor man's vision of the Lady of Guadalupe. I was struck by how lowly, insignificant people have to beg the church to regard them with the esteem with which God regards them. We are not sure whether Mary appeared in a vision to this poor man. Perhaps we have our Protestant doubts. Yet even if we question the vision, the tragic truth remains: The poor and lowly often have to beg the church to proclaim and live out its message of a merciful, compassionate God! Behind the vision's gilded cactus leaves, miraculous roses and imprinted cloak is the longing for a God who comes, not in the might of military conquest nor in the ecclesiastical forms and evangelism plans of a mighty church, but in simple, compassionate respect and regard for the lowly, the uneducated, the hungry, the women, the poor, the children.

We sing the Magnificat to comfort the lowly. We sing to put ourselves in solidarity with the lowly and those who suffer. We sing in order to bring in the reign and community of our Lord Jesus Christ.

To strengthen our faith. Finally, we sing Mary's song to strengthen our own faith. We keep announcing to one another the sort of God in which we believe: a God who has respect for the Marys of Nazareth, for vulnerable, pregnant, unmarried women; a God who rummages through the dump with the hungry; a God who cries when children are killed and women are raped; a God who sees visions with poor farmers and plants roses on their hillsides.

The successful outcome of this conference will be determined not so much by the confirmation of our theological positions as by the faith of the folks who sit around this table, by the kind of God we believe in as we talk together. Luther said that Mary sang the Magnificat on the basis of her experience of being enlightened and instructed by the Holy Spirit. We pray that this meeting might be the schoolroom of the Holy Spirit.

Bonnie Jensen, Chapel Talk in Mexico City

Music is a Gift of God

I wish to see all arts, principally music, in the service of God who gave and created them. Music is a fair and glorious gift of God. I would not for the world forgo my humble share of music. Singers are never sorrowful but are merry and smile through their troubles in song. Music makes people kinder, gentler, more staid and reasonable. I am strongly persuaded that after theology there is no art that can be placed on a level with music; for besides theology, music is the only art capable of affording peace and joy of the heart...the devil flees before the sound of music almost as much as before the Word of God.

Martin Luther

Harold Nielsen, 67, leaned on one knee, with tears in his eyes, and tried to explain what he'd seen in Mexico. "The second day in Cuernavaca you wake up at 3 A.M. and start to cry," he said. "You don't have to go to the university to see that something is wrong."

Henry Bellars

> PSALM 100 : 1-2
>
> *Make a joyful noise to the Lord, all the lands! Serve the Lord with gladness! Come into his presence with singing!*

REFLECTION • ACTION

1. Have you experienced grief over injustice and pain inflicted on others? Has it ever caused you to weep? If so, what follows your weeping? How can the church recapture its capacity to grieve?

2. Has music helped you in your struggle? If so, how? What songs (music) seem to minister most powerfully to you? Thank someone today who has given a gift of music. If possible sing to someone you visit in the hospital or in prison. Find lyrics that express Jesus' concern for justice. Learn the song *Ubi Caritas*, below.

3. Memorize a verse or two of a new hymn during each liturgical season. Sing it on the way to work or school. Sing songs together as table prayers. Learn songs from other nations and cultures.

4. Some good music and worship resources are: *Bread for the Journey*, Edited by Ruth C. Duck, Pilgrim Press, 1981; *Banquet of Praise*, by Bread for the World, 1990; *Global Songs #1 and #2*, and *Songs of Faith and Liberation from Around the World*, Augsburg Press, 1996 *Music from Taize*, Responses, Litanies, Acclamation, Canons, Volumes 1 and 2, Collins Liturgical Press, 1986; *Hymns Reimaged*, by Mirian Theresa Winter and The Medical Mission Sisters from *The Other Side*, 1-800-700-9280.

Ubi Caritas, from Taize

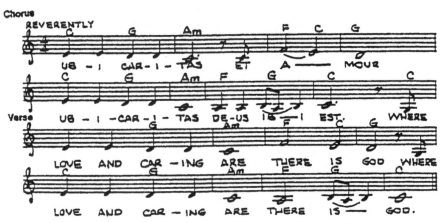

(based on I John 4:7)

REFLECTION AND DISCOVERY

WHERE IS DADDY?

FROM CHARITY TO JUSTICE

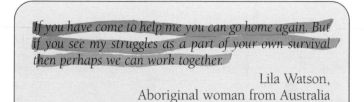

If you have come to help me you can go home again. But if you see my struggles as a part of your own survival then perhaps we can work together.

Lila Watson,
Aboriginal woman from Australia

Most people want to help the hungry. They will respond to scenes of starving babies' bloated bellies and mothers who have to choose which child will get food and which will die because there isn't enough food for both. Requests for offerings to help provide relief for the hungry are usually successful. It is not difficult to raise funds for starving people whether the appeal is local or global.

Years ago my wife and I held off getting our first color television for a long time. Pressure from our teenage daughters prompted us to take the plunge. We looked for the best buy. Then one morning our oldest daughter came down for breakfast and said, "Why don't we take the money for our color TV and give it to our church's hunger appeal instead." I was pleasantly surprised, almost blown away. After carefully asking some questions to find out where the change of attitude came from, I discovered that the night before she had watched a TV program put on by World Vision. Seeing children suffer and die for lack of nourishment moved her to tears and she wanted to do something about it. Whenever the hunger crisis gets the attention of the media, offerings go up. People want to help.

Most agencies working to alleviate hunger in the world are involved in relief (fund-raising), education (information) and advocacy (working for needed changes). While I was the director of my church's hunger program I found that most people are comfortable with an appeal for money; however, a careful analysis revealed that the average gift per year to the hunger appeal was less than the cost of one hamburger. But it was alright to ask for money.

On the other hand, learning about the root causes of hunger and the need for changes in the way the world was ordered was not very popular.

Working for justice is more complex but very important if we really want to help. The appeal for charity (feeling sorry and sharing our resources) is the beginning, a good starting place, but it is only the first step in the fight against the evil of hunger. Of course, I wanted to affirm our daughter's desire to give some money to the hunger appeal; what I found challenging was to help her move from charity to justice, prophetic justice.

There is a saying that helps to explain this challenge to work for justice, not just for charity. It goes like this: "If people are hungry you can give them some fish and they will live another day. It's called relief. But if you not only give a fish, but teach them how to fish for themselves they will be helped to feed themselves in the future." This is often called development. That sounds good but it can be misleading if it is not followed with the next step. There is a third part of that saying that is critical to our efforts to move beyond guilt. We must not only offer the fish (relief) and assistance in knowing how to fish themselves (development), but we must move over in the pond and give them a place to fish. Or as someone has added, we must stop polluting the pond where they fish and give them a fair price for their fish. This third step has many facets to it. It is called working for justice, fairness. Justice includes efforts to end oppression and unfair practices of what Walter Wink calls the domination system. Moving from charity to justice is difficult because it calls for careful listening, increased awareness and critical thinking about the attitudes and values that have brought us to this current crisis.

While a graduate student at the School of Theology in Claremont, CA, I took a semester course called "World Hunger and Christian Response." It was an eye-opener for me because I was still in the charity phase of my growth. Dean Freudenberger, an agronomist, Methodist, clergyman and missionary to Africa, was my teacher. We studied the different things that have brought about poverty, hunger and oppression such as:

1. RESOURCE ABUSE – the exploitation of land, water, air and women

2. NEO COLONIALISM – the continuation of domination and control over poorer countries

3. TECHNOLOGY GAP – benefits and limitations of technology

4. TRADE AND AID – who sets the rules and when is aid harmful

5. MILITARISM – the effects of war (arms race) on the environment and national priorities

6. TRANSNATIONAL CORPORATIONS – the drive for profits versus the voice of the prophets, globalization issues

7. POPULATION BOMB – how can we feed growing populations in the world

8. DISPELLING MYTHS – exposing misconceptions and Band-Aid efforts

9. SUSTAINABLE AGRICULTURE – the integrity and care of creation

10. GRASSROOTS PARTICIPATION – partnership rather than top-down development

It is a mistake to take one of these components and work as though it alone will solve the problem. We need to encourage efforts at all levels even when we are heavily involved in one particular issue. A good book by David Beckmann and Arthur Simon called *Grace at the Table* helps to illuminate the various issues involved in working for justice as well as charity. It is an updating of Simon's book called *Bread for the World* that came out in 1974. Every church library should have a copy because it makes a good adult forum study guide. Another well-documented book recently published by Food First is *The Paradox of Plenty,* edited by Douglas Boucher.

There is another set of root causes regarding hunger and oppression that has to do with the theology, preaching and teaching in our churches. This might be called the underdevelopment of theology or the captivity of the church to cultural values. It includes:

1. NEGLECT OF THE SCRIPTURES – What we see or don't see in the scriptures is often influenced by our economics of privilege and ties to the empire.

2. NEGLECT OF STEWARDSHIP – Creation and our management of it is overshadowed by our strong human redemption-centered theology.

3. NEGLECT OF COMMUNITY – Strong individualism gives the personal aspects of salvation too much attention and discourages global awareness and responsibility for others.

4. NEGLECT OF THE PROPHETIC – In many subtle ways we have silenced the prophetic voice while emphasizing grace without responsibility.

5. NEGLECT OF CONVERSION – We have been too timid to call for a

change in our lives and sidestepped the radical aspects of the call to follow Jesus.

6. NEGLECT OF ECONOMICS – The church needs to be aware of the origin and significance of wealth as it relates to faithful living, and what greed has done to relationships.

7. NEGLECT OF CRITICAL THINKING –We have not encouraged questions that can lead to analysis, growth and change.

8. NEGLECT OF THE POOR – Jesus and all of scripture give far more attention to the poor than is given in current theological training and preaching.

9. NEGLECT OF RELEVANT WORSHIP – Lament and struggle needs to be balanced with the transcendant and praise. Worship that is boring or mere performance is not true worship.

10. NEGLECT OF DISCIPLESHIP TRAINING – Too much energy is given to maintenance of the institution rather than equipping laity for engaging the principalities and powers.

The scriptures are full of the call for justice. Von Rad says there is no concept more important in the Hebrew scriptures than justice. When Isaiah called the people of Israel to repent and come back to their covenant relationship with Yahweh, they were reminded that it would mean seeking justice and correcting oppression (1:17): letting the oppressed go free, breaking every yoke (58:6). Micah spells out what God is really looking for, what God requires or expects from those who have covenanted to be a blessing. "What does the Lord require of you but to do justice, love kindness and walk humbly with your God (6:8)." In Luke, Jesus sets out his agenda, his purpose and his message of salvation. It included the mission of justice, "The Spirit has sent me to let the oppressed go free (4:18)." In Matthew Jesus reminds the religious leaders that they had given too much attention to ritual purity and neglected the weightier matter of justice (23:23).

For us to address the issue of oppression will sometimes involve conflict and resistance. The Old Testament prophet Amos was told to go home, go preach somewhere else when he talked about greed and oppression of the poor. In the Exodus story Moses was called by God to help the oppressed Israelites who had been made slaves in Egypt. Moses was not sent to bring relief such as food, better tools and blankets, important as they were. He was told to go to Pharaoh, the powers of domination and say, "Let my people go." It met stiff resistance. (See Exodus 3ff.) Even his own people complained and preferred the good old days.

It can be discouraging to work for justice. One needs to find ways to continually be renewed and energized. Finding a small group to meet with on a regular basis is important. Alfred Krass in his magazine article in *The Other Side* gives some helpful hints about how to avoid burn out and cynicism. He suggests that pastors should learn to lead, not coerce their congregations into dramatic changes; recognize that meaningful change takes years; help people find new meaning in old symbols and language; avoid pontificating; speak to people's hearts; always give a word of hope; and remember that experience is the best teacher. I would also add that music is important to staying alive and positive. Always be on the alert to find music that keeps one grounded in this world but lifts our spirits.

Ezekiel 16:49

This was the guilt of your sister Sodom: she and her daughters had pride, excess of food and prosperous ease, but did not aid the poor and needy.

Psalm 82:1-4

God has taken his place in the divine council; in the midst of the gods he holds judgment. How long will you judge unjustly and show partiality to the wicked? Give justice to the weak and the orphan; maintain the right of the lowly and the destitute. Rescue the weak and the needy; deliver them from the hand of the wicked.

REFLECTION • ACTION

1. What cultural values need to be challenged if we are to move from charity to justice issues? What theological assumptions or perceptions need challenging?

2. When might giving aid actually be doing more harm than good? Discuss or think about the meaning behind the opening quote from Lila Watson.

3. Suggest a letter writing campaign by your faith community. Get information and help to do letter writing from Bread for the World or
   your church's public policy office. Contact Bread for the World toll free
   at 1-888-297-2767. Join a CROP hunger walk.

4. Read *Christian Faith and Public Policy* by Arthur Simon, Eerdmans,
   1987; and/or *To Act Justly, Love Tenderly, Work Humbly*, by Walter
   Brueggemann, Sharon Parks and Thomas H. Groome, Paulist Press
   1986; and/or *Binding the Strong Man*-A Political Reading of Mark's
   Gospel by Ched Myers, Orbis, 1997; and/or *The Paradox of Plenty*,
   edited by Douglas Boucher, Food First Books, 1999.

FROM PRIVATE TO SOCIAL CONSCIENCE

> *The Christian life, while intensely personal, is always communal...The privatization of piety is not part of the Christian tradition and it undermines the Christian life...Christian spirituality is, therefore, the spirituality of Christian community. But it is not Christian community lived in isolation from the world.*
>
> John deGruchy

One of Cesar Chavez's children was reminiscing about his childhood. Having the leader of the United Farm Workers as his father was not easy for him. There were many things he regretted about the way things were in his family. But one thing he said he will always treasure from his childhood is that his father helped him develop a social conscience.

How many of us have helped our children develop a social conscience? How do you do that? What is a social conscience?

Most of us are bothered with a bad conscience when we personally have committed sins that hurt a neighbor or friend. If I lie to someone or commit adultery, my conscience tells me I have sinned. Conscience is an inner voice that reminds me that a violation has taken place. A person without a conscience is a danger to society.

The trouble is that too often our conscience is trained to be sensitive to individual violations of God's law but not very well trained to be sensitive to social or corporate sins. As a result we are more easily convicted, for example, when we are reminded about behavior toward a spouse than when we are reminded about human rights being denied the poor as a result of corporate, military, or government action.

Individual sins receive far more attention in sermons and Christian literature than do social sins. Our rugged individualism and personal piety may allow us to dismiss ourselves from any corporate guilt or shame. Yet some of the injustices inflicted on people are not attributed to any one person but to a society that has allowed it to happen. We may allow corporate systems to be greedy for us but feel no guilt.

A social conscience is one that is trained to identify with society in accepting responsibility for injustice done to groups of people. It accepts the social and corporate nature of our lives as well as the uniqueness of the individual. It is able to make connections between larger societal problems and personal decisions we make. A social conscience is a part of what we call compassion. It motivates and energizes us to care about groups of people in more than a superficial way. By it we are united with those who suffer and are able to respond more wisely.

When I was a seminary student we drew numbers in the spring to see who would get first choice of rooms in the dormitory in the fall. I drew a bad number. So I came back later, pretending I hadn't drawn a number yet. This time I was much higher in the draft. No one questioned my clever maneuver. It awarded me one of the best rooms for my senior year.

But that night my conscience bothered me so much I couldn't sleep. I had cheated. How could I be a pastor if I would do things like that, I thought. All night I tossed and turned. So the next day I went to the dean of housing and confessed what I had done. It was a relief to be forgiven. During that time in my life my conscience was very sensitive to individual and personal sins. It would lead me to confession and reconciliation on a personal level. Confession at Sunday worship always focused on individual sins.

I remember going that same week to hear Martin Luther King Jr. He talked about the sin of racism. At first he referred only to the bus boycott in Montgomery, Alabama. I thought, how could humans be so inhumane. Then he went on to talk about racism in the North...in the Twin Cities where I lived. He talked about corporate racism and institutional racism. My eyes were opened to the many ways in which prejudice is present in all of us. I began to see the violence of racism.

As I rode back to the seminary with my classmates, we discussed the statistics and facts that made us more aware of racism in our own backyard. We realized that we belonged to a society that was just as racist as the people of Montgomery. But that night I didn't lose any sleep because of a bad conscience. I slept like a baby. There was no inner need to confess my sins to anyone. My conscience was not as sensitive to social sins as it was to my individual sins. Since then my social conscience has been enlightened. Now

I am more apt to be concerned about violations that are corporate and social. I read my *Bible* differently. The prophets and Jesus called for repentance for both individual and social sins.

OTHER VOICES

The story of Hagar and Sarah in Genesis is about the economic stratification of women as much as it is about ethnic discrimination of one woman against another. Translated into today's language, Hagar was a domestic; Sarah was her employer. No race or culture has a monopoly on evil. At some point, virtually every culture has, if not instituted slavery, then profited from the bartering of human flesh.

Renita Weems, *Just a Sister Away*

ISAIAH 6:4-5

And the foundations of the threshold shook at the voice of him who called, and the house was filled with smoke. And I said: ""Woe is me! For I am lost; for I am a man of unclean lips, and I dwell in the midst of a people of unclean lips; for my eyes have seen the King, the Lord of hosts.

REFLECTION • ACTION

1. What has helped you develop a social conscience, a sensitivity to the corporate nature and extent of injustice done to people?

2. What can be done to help children develop a social as well as individual conscience? Can public education contribute to this? What can congregations do? Parents do? Visit a children's book store for help.

3. Pick a play or movie that helps to raise social justice awareness. Invite a friend to see it with you. Talk to a teacher about how textbooks, curriculum and global education can help students develop a social conscience and global awareness.

4. Read *Families Valued,* Parenting and Politics for the Good of all People by Jack Nelson-Pallmeyer, Friendship Press, 1996; and/or *Engaging the Powers* by Walter Wink, Fortress Press 1992; and/or *Revolution and Renewal* by Tony Campolo, Westminster John Knox Press, 2000.

FROM IGNORANCE TO DISCOVERY

> *Discovery is not always a joyful process. It sometimes involves struggle, pain and confusion. The very essence of discovering is embracing the unknown, loving the confusion as well as the certainty. Discovering is not only about creating harmonies; it also means being with the disharmonies. To trust the discovering process is an act of great courage.*
>
> Don Christensen

Life is filled with moments of learning and discovery. Watch a baby discover its fingers. How fascinating it is to observe the changes that take place when the teenager in your family first discovers sexual attraction. Church members often come alive when the Christian community helps them discover gifts they never thought they had. Discovery can be exhilarating and life-changing. It also can be painful.

Learning about human suffering can be laden with heaviness unless it is experienced from the perspective of a grace filled Christian community. Then we begin to see that it is my sister, my brother, who suffers. When one from among my family becomes a victim, I want to know. St. Paul writes "when one member suffers, we all suffer."

Many Christians have found that face-to-face encounters with people who suffer is the best way to discover what the reality is and how we can respond. It can happen while riding a bus to work, when serving food at a soup kitchen, when visiting with a refugee family, or while on a trip to places where people live in poverty and oppression.

A group leader said to those about to embark on a journey into a poverty situation, "Be ready to meet Jesus in the faces of those you encounter." In the debriefing after the trip, one person commented, "God is trying to say something to us today and is saying it through those in poverty. I wonder if we are able to listen?"

Like seeking Jesus in the face of another, listening also is a key to discovery. So many of our biases, stereotypes and fears are the result of not being with people long enough to listen to them. When people know they have been listened to, they receive a sense of dignity and power. As listeners we also experience a new relationship with those who suffer. We are empowered. Healing begins when we have taken time to listen, not just to words spoken, but to feelings, atmosphere, questioning, hopes and circumstances.

OTHER VOICES

It Started in the Milk Barn

I had been milking in the barn, thinking about the irony of producing too much milk while people in the world were hungry, when I remembered an invitation in our church bulletin for people interested in representing our conference on a study tour in Mexico. The announcement said the purpose was to explore the root causes of world hunger.

God seemed to be urging me to go and so I sent in my name, never dreaming that I would be selected. The reality of poverty, and the faith of those Mexican Christians living in the midst of it, changed my life.

When I returned home, this basically shy person – one whom the teachers in high school urged to participate more in classes – began to speak and even preach sermons in other churches throughout the Lakeshore Conference in Southern Wisconsin. Even more exciting was to speak to congregations of other denominations and various non-church groups.

My church has been supportive of my efforts. We have sponsored a hunger meal and a Seder supper on Maundy Thursday. Currently we have an ongoing program of donating one penny per day from each person to our church's hunger appeal. People are discovering that there is more to it than charity.

Most important, others have caught the vision of ending world hunger. Another person in my 240-baptized-member congregation has served as coordinator of our local interfaith food pantry.

Sometimes when I am in the barn, milking the cows and thus producing even more surplus milk, I have to think and laugh. When I went to Mexico two years ago, I agreed to work on hunger issues for one year. I found I have a lifetime commitment.

Marilyn Borchardt, Wisconsin Farmer

Thinking Differently about Economic Anthropology

A theological task is to begin to think differently about our economic culture, beginning with our economic anthropology. We are so deeply socialized into the assumptions of modern capitalism concerning money, work, value…that it is difficult for us to even entertain perspectives that originate from different assumptions such as the *Bible*'s. But unless we 'think outside the box,' we will remain captive to the idolatrous (and circular) logic of capitalism, namely that ultimately all power flows both to and from capital.

Ched Myers

David Bosch, in his book *Transforming Mission*, quotes Howard Snyder: "Kingdom people seek first the Kingdom of God and its justice; church people often put church work above concerns for justice, mission and truth. Church people think about how to get people into the church; kingdom people think about how to get the church into the world. Church people worry that the world might change the church; kingdom people work to see the church change the world."

Howard Snyder

MATTHEW 25:37-40

Then the righteous will answer him, "Lord, when did we see you hungry and feed you, or thirsty and give you drink? And when did we see you a stranger and welcome you, or naked and clothe you? And when did we see you sick or in prison and visit you?" And the King will answer them, "Truly, I say to you, as you did it to one of the least of these my brethren, you did it to me."

EXODUS 2:11

One day, when Moses had grown up, he went out to his people and looked on their burdens; and he saw an Egyptian beating a Hebrew, one of his people.

REFLECTION • ACTION

1. The word "conscientization" refers to experiencing the reality of human suffering, then making the connection between suffering and its various linkages to other issues and the call for justice. To be con-scientized is to be awakened and be doing something toward human liberation, either for oneself or for others. What discovery experiences have helped to conscientize you about various kinds of oppression that cause human suffering?

2. Subscribe to a periodical that will keep you in touch with justice discoveries and happenings in the Third World, not often covered in the mass media. Some suggestions are: *Prism* Evangelicals for Social Action, Box 473, 10 E. Landcaster, Waynewood, PA 19096; *The New Internationalist*, Box 1143, Lewiston, NY, 14092; *The Other Side*, 300 W. Apsley St., Philadelphia, PA 19144; *Alternatives*, 5312 Mornignside Ave, Box 2857, Sioux City, IA 51106; *The National Catholic Reporter*, Box 423, MT Morris, IL 61054; *Food First* 398 60th ST, Oakland, CA 94618; *Sojourners,* 2401 15th Street, NW, Washington DC 20009, *Amnesty International*, 322 8th Ave., NYC, NY 10001

3. Read *Just Generosity* A New Vision for Overcoming Poverty in America, by Ron Sider, Baker Books, 1999; and/or *The Quickening of America* by Frances Moore Lappe and Paul Martin DuBois, Jossey-Bass Inc. Publishers, 1994; and/or *Politics, Religion and the Common Good* by Martin Marty with Jonathan Moore, Jossey-Bass, 2000.

FACE-TO-FACE ENCOUNTERS

In our efforts to respond to the needs of poor and hungry people with compassion and integrity, there is no good substitute for face-to-face encounters with the people we wish to help. Avoiding poor people is easy in our culture. Even people who want to reach out may find themselves blocked by fear.

In *Evangelism and the Poor*: a Biblical Challenge for the Church, authors George S. Johnson and Ana de Garcia suggest some ways of meeting hurting people and learning about their needs. Pick one or two as your commitment for this next phase of your faith journey. Let your life make a difference.

1. Volunteer to help at a food pantry or soup kitchen two times during the next few weeks. This will include entering into conversation with the recipients where appropriate.

2. Volunteer (with others) to weatherize the home or paint the house of a poor family or elderly person(s) and get to know the residents. Offer your service with Habitat for Humanity.

3. Visit and observe at an emergency center for the disenfranchised. Examples might include the emergency waiting room at your county hospital, the courthouse where hearings and trials take place, the food-stamp center, the legal aid office, center for abused women and children, or shelters for the homeless. Affirm people who are trying to make a difference.

4. Arrange a visit to talk with those working with drug and alcohol addiction; and/or mentally ill homeless people.

5. Volunteer to go with a social worker or police officer on visits that will help you understand the struggles of the people without resources to cope. Talk to a conscientized real estate representative or mortgage officer about fear, prejudice and issues related to equality of opportunities in your area.

6. Spend a night (from 10:00 P.M. until 5:00 A.M.) on the streets of an inner city, to listen, touch, taste, smell and feel what goes on and how some people of our society live. (This should be done in pairs or as a group.)

7. Go on a mini (weekend or weeklong) trip to a Third-World situation where face-to-face encounter with the poor is possible. Contact Center for Global Education in Minnesota (1-800-229-8889) or Third World Opportunities in California (1-619-449-9381) or Ministry of Money in Maryland (301-428-9560) or Journey Into Freedom in Oregon (503-244-4728) or your church's mission office.

8. Arrange for two visits with a refugee or displaced family, one in your home, one in their home, to discuss their struggles, culture, values, and signs of hope.

9. Visit an Indian reservation and arrange for in-depth conversations with Native Americans and those who work with them. If possible, stay overnight.

10. Visit a prison on two different occasions and enter into dialogue with inmates, with a special focus on abuse, poverty, racism, societal prejudice, and prison reform.

11. Visit with two farm families who have experienced foreclosure. Seek understanding and give support. Discover the issues facing agriculture today and learn how all of us are connected.

12. Take time to listen to nature and our environment as it cries out for liberation from exploitation. Ask an environmentalist to take you on a trip that will help you better understand what's happening and why.

13. Offer to help those suffering from HIV-AIDS. Learn what their challenges and options are.

14. Spend time on location where older people hang out, especially those who have no family support. Listen to their stories.

15. Become a mentor or big brother/sister to a child. Help a youth at risk with homework or go with them to their court appearance. Invite some one to talk to your church (group) about child abuse and teen violence.

16. Go with a group (youth or adult) to visit rural America. Shalom Hill Farm in MN offers interaction with farmers, clergy, environmentalists, activists and other resource persons. Retreat facilities available, call (507) 831-2232.

FROM GUILT TO RESPONSIBILITY

> *One of our problems today is that law and gospel have fallen apart. We rarely challenge ourselves by presenting high standards of personal living. Hence we rarely proclaim the "law" in an effective way. We do not want to make people feel guilty. In regard to personal life our effort is to reassure and comfort. On the other hand, some of us do sometimes proclaim law. But we rarely connect this law to personal life.*
>
> John B. Cobb, Jr.
> *Grace and Responsibility*

No feeling is more common to those who learn of the global atrocities inflicted on the poor and powerless than the feeling of guilt. Almost everyone who learns of the millions dying of hunger feels guilty about our overabundance and waste. Guilt can be painful, disturbing, even debilitating. Sometimes we avoid issues that cause guilt feelings because we prefer tranquility and peace of mind. On other occasions the feeling of guilt leads us to compensate with hyperactivity, that is, endless doing to avoid feeling guilty. At best, guilt is a motivator, and like any feeling, it is healthy, given due and appropriate attention. Left to itself, however, it does little to sustain us in the long haul.

Perhaps some of us have been too quick to write off guilt as unhealthy and destructive. If we avoid anything that triggers our guilt without distinguishing between healthy, normal guilt and false, destructive guilt, we are ignoring a deeper reality in creation. Guilt can protect us from irresponsible action. The sting of conscience reminds us that lying is wrong, not because God commanded against it but because it negates life.

Two factors are important to consider. First we must learn, as the article *The*

Gift of Guilt (below) suggests, to distinguish between authentic and inauthentic, good and bad guilt. Inauthentic guilt focuses on how bad and how powerless we are, rather than on action we can take or behavior we can change. Authentic guilt produces repentance and invites us to make contact with whomever we have hurt. It leads to responsible action.

Feeling healthy, authentic guilt is a gift which prepares us for repentance, forgiveness and reconciliation. When reports of injustice and exploitation only lead us to avoid or be rid of guilt, we may miss an important word God is saying to us. Many of us have been raised to view guilt negatively, yet its gift is to lead us to positive, creative action, and above all, to responsibility. Even when we convince ourselves that we are not guilty, we remain responsible.

In *Covenanted Self*, Walter Brueggemann suggests that we have sidestepped the element of responsibility and obedience in the Christian life partly because of a distorted "free grace." He says Luther's inserting "alone" in his reading of apostle Paul's theology of grace has resulted in a failure to see how the gospel is both "profoundly unconditional and massively conditional." In preaching obedience (responsibly) Brueggemann encourages us to see the commandments of love for God and love for neighbor as "disciplines essential to the revolution." I have found this theme in Brueggemann's *The Covenanted Self* as well as *Interpretation and Obedience* to be both disturbingly provocative and energizing.

Frederick Buechner gives another dimension to the meaning of responsibility when he says in his excellent book, *The Longing For Home*, "when Jesus commanded us to love our neighbors as ourselves, it was not just for our neighbors' sake that He commanded it, but for our own sakes as well. Not to help find some way to feed the children who are starving to death is to have some precious part of who we are starve to death with them."

OTHER VOICES

The Gift of Guilt

Guilt is a uniquely human response; without it we would be less than wholly accountable for our lives. Genuine guilt is an arousal of the heart, an alarm that warns us of a wound for which we are responsible. Such guilt is a gift, a gift that alerts us to an injured relationship – with a friend, with God, with our own best hopes and deepest values. As psychologist Willard Gaylin observes, guilt is the guardian of our goodness.

The challenge for each of us is to learn to distinguish authentic guilt from its pernicious false cousins. In genuine guilt we honor our responsibility for a relationship to which we are committed. This becomes a grace as it alerts us to those concrete actions by which we have injured others or undermined values. Here my sense of guilt – painful as it may be – is the first step on the Christian journey of repentance, forgiveness and reconciliation. In the daily conversions through which we grow in love and faith, genuine guilt often is our guide.

But though guilt is meant to be a grace that leads to healing, we know that too often it is instead a curse. The painful arousal seems to go awry; this guardian of our goodness becomes a monster that takes up residence to torment us and distract us from reconciliation. This destructive guilt often arises when we allow ourselves to become victims of external pressures and exaggerated ideals. We then feel wretched for not meeting our own expectations (I feel guilty for not being "the perfect spouse"), or those of other people (I blame myself for not achieving the kind of success my parents had hoped for).

False guilt lures us from a focus on what we have done to an absorption with how bad we are. The mood moves from "I have failed here" to "I am a failure." In this maelstrom of defeat, I lose sight of the particular behaviors that I can and should change. I even lose sight of the relationship that I have injured. Increasingly, the focus is on me – my wretchedness, my failure, my pain. When I succumb to the temptation to "entertain" these painful feelings, I give this disruptive mood power over me. The gift of guilt becomes a curse, and reconciliation escapes me.

Initially, most of us are understandably reluctant to share responsibility for the ancient and continuing injustice in human affairs. "I am not personally to blame," we protest, "for poverty or slavery or terrorism." But maturity brings many of us to acknowledge that we belong to and are active members of this wounded and wounding species. We need less and less to deny our involvement in this shared history of sin and guilt. This need not lead us to wallow in a mood of hopelessness and self-pity. The recognition of original guilt can instead bring us to a tolerance that is blessed with patience. And it turns us, as believers, to our God who does not cease to forgive even such a race. This original guilt, too, is a "bad feeling" that is good for us to know.

Guilt becomes a gift only through the development of a mature conscience. Children do not easily distinguish genuine guilt from false; adolescents often are hard pressed to separate conformity to other people's expectations from the pursuit of authentic values. Only the well-seasoned conscience of the mature Christian adult can discern the face and feel of genuine guilt. This guilt is a precious gift; it alerts us to our failings and impels us to seek the healing grace of repentance and reconciliation.

Evelyn Eaton Whitehead and
James D. Whitehead

Brokenness-Blaming-Responsibility

Evil truly exists. It is incompleteness and active brokenness springing from incompleteness, the parts that have not yet been put to right. Evil is still a real choice; our brokenness can cause us to work against God. God doesn't want that. We are called to be light, not agents of the night. But neither are we to shoulder the blame for the creation of darkness and neither is God. We are all responsible for growing beyond it. We are responsible to heal what we can, and limit the damage of what remains enslaved to the void. This is the proper boundary of human responsibilty.

Bill Williams in *Naked Before God*

So let's not wallow in our guilt – but let's not ignore it either. There are many things in today's world for us to feel guilty about. Praise God that Christians know what's to be done with guilt and know the power that can change the situations that give birth to it.

Charles Lutz
Editor: *God, Goods and the Common Good*

ISAIAH 1:17-18

Learn to do good; seek justice, correct oppression; defend the fatherless, plead for the widow. "Come now, let us reason together," says the Lord: "though your sins are like scarlet, they shall be as white as snow; though they are red like crimson, they shall become like wool."

REFLECTION • ACTION

1. What role has guilt played in the development of a social conscience for you? How does one discern good from bad guilt in a practical way?

2. How can people be helped who seem to avoid honest encounter with the reality of human suffering because they don't want to feel guilty? Think about and discuss the quote from John Cobb, Jr. and the article by the Whiteheads.

3. Find a few like-minded friends with whom you can talk freely about authentic guilt and corporate guilt. Allow your conversation to be part of the healing process. Organize a support group around global justice issues or around one issue. Watch for interconnectedness.

4. Read *The Covenanted Self,* Explorations in Law and Covenant, by Walter Brueggemann, Fortress Press, 1999; and/or *Grace and Responsibilty* by John Cobb, Jr., Abington Press, 1995; and/or *The Longing For Home* by Frederick Buechner, Harper, 1996.

FROM BLAMING TO ANALYSIS

"Conventional wisdom" focuses on the victims of hunger and always sees them as people lacking something – food and money, of course, but also technology, skills, knowledge (and, in the worst cases, even intelligence). What if, on the contrary, we regarded these millions of poor people as a rich national resource who lack only power, the power to control their own environments and the circumstances of their lives? By upending it, we shall discover that the problem of hunger is not one of technology or organization but of politics; morally, the issue is not charity, but justice.

Susan George

Entering into discussion with people about why there is this or that suffering in the world can be discouraging and confusing. Some people sound so convincing. Then you hear someone else name causes that are entirely different. Who do you believe? Trust? Then you learn that symptoms are different than causes. Does it really make any difference what analysis you work from in responding to the cries of human suffering? Can the average person really understand the complexity of causes?

Without appropriate analysis there are some tendencies that, when followed, lead to powerlessness and a continuation of things as they are. It seems natural, for example, to "blame the victim" when tragedy and suffering happens. If only they will change, then things will improve. The problem is "over there." So we send volunteers, aid, researchers and technicians to work with the victims and their environment. However, careful analysis and testimony of knowledgeable witnesses may teach us that some of the causes reach out beyond the victims or the country in which they live.

Another tendency is to accept simplistic explanations of something that is very complex. For example, it may be true that overpopulation is causing increased stress on the earth's ability to produce enough food, but it is simplistic to suggest that if we convinced people to have fewer babies there wouldn't be hunger in the world. Population growth needs to be addressed, but along with other issues or it becomes a scapegoat. By checking facts about food surpluses, economic opportunities and inadequate distribution we'd see that the simple answers, in this case fewer babies, ultimately is no answer at all. Or, it is often easier to live with natural disaster as the cause than to hear that the relationship of power and control among people is more central to the analysis.

The Mennonite Central Committee made a clear witness about analysis when they said, "The need is not for short-termed relief, but the opportunity to create a more just society, where the poor will have access to the resources needed for food security and self-reliance."

We also tend to gravitate toward explanations that favor our position of privilege. If it fits our economic or theological bias we are more apt to sit up and listen. We all have our golden calves, those ideals or idols we have grown up with which may not deserve the worship and uncritical allegiance we give them. In moving from blaming to analysis, we need a willingness to look at how others see the problem, especially those who are the victims.

Analysis requires that we look at economic, political and social causes behind the never-ending injustices that cause human suffering. When we observe progress and growth, we need to ask: at what cost and for whom has this program been accomplished? People of faith need to look at theological root causes as well (see page 43). It is easy to blame sin but what is the sin? The *Bible* seems to suggest that oppression, not laziness, is the main cause of poverty. God's people are called to correct oppression as well as give charity (Isaiah 1:17). See chapter seven on From Charity to Justice.

It takes considerable effort to probe behind the images of starving babies, disappearing family farms, polluted rivers and lakes, and homeless people to discover the root causes. To move beyond guilt and powerlessness, it is necessary to move from easy answers to analysis, from blaming others to seeing how we all contribute to the process of oppression. Without proper analysis we may end up hurting the very people we want to help.

OTHER VOICES

The Good Samaritan Revisited

Around the biblical parable of the Good Samaritan, with the addition of three or four commentaries, all of which are apocryphal, we understand our role not just theologically, but politically as well. It is this parable that Christians in the Philippines use to justify working within the struggle for liberation.

In the pre-political interpretation, the story is simple. There is the victim. A priest passes by. A Levite passes by on the way to worship. The Good Samaritan comes and we are told in the *Bible* that his heart melted. No theological motive, just compassion. That is how a Christian should love.

The model the Christian is given for loving is the Good Samaritan who helps the victim. But that is in very personal, individual terms. How does it become political? First, how does it become social?

According to the first apocryphal story, the Good Samaritan came week after week and found victim after victim. He said, "Here is a problem. It is no longer an individual problem. This is a social problem. It needs a social response." True to his good nature and his political limitation, he went around to his fellow Samaritans and collected money to set up a Good Samaritan hospital. Because there are very many victims, you need an institutional response to an increasing number of victims.

But it is not quite political yet. It becomes political because, when you put up an institution like a hospital, you have to hire staff. And you have to have staff-development seminars. When you have staff-development seminars, they start analyzing, "Why are there so many victims?"

According to the janitor: "It is simple. Like you ask me: Why is the corridor always wet? It is because someone has failed to turn off the leaking tap." There are many victims because someone is causing those victims. Oh, the robbers! That is the first lesson in politics. Not to see only victims, but to see a robber.

Normally the church sees victims, helps victims. Sees robber and says, "Don't rob again." Robber says, "I have problems. My children need money, they are into drugs." The church can help the victim and help the robber and see that they both need help.

According to the second apocryphal story, one day the Good Samaritan came one hour earlier. Instead of seeing only the victim, he saw the robber robbing the victim. The victim was not yet the victim. He was resisting. The Good Samaritan says, "I still must love: But how do you love? That is the problem."

Why do we look at ourselves as the Good Samaritan? Couldn't we be the victim? Couldn't we be the robber? Why is Christian morality associated with the Good Samaritan? What is the Good Samaritan politically?

The Good Samaritan politically is in the middle, not quite robber, not quite victim, not yet oppressor, not yet oppressed, not very rich, not very poor either. We are in the middle, where most of us want to believe that we are. Not involved but feeling the need to get involved. Because that is the ethical call to act. Once you see that, the call is to love. To love in a conflict situation is to take sides. Once you take sides, your next dilemma is, How far do you go?

Father Ed de la Torre

Oppression – The Cause of Poverty

For the *Bible*, oppression is the basic cause of poverty, but I want also to introduce a middle term that sheds some light: despoliation, or theft. In other words, the oppressor steals from the oppressed and impoverishes them. The oppressed are therefore those who have been impoverished, for while the oppressor oppresses the poor because they are poor and powerless, the poor have become poor in the first place because they have been oppressed. The principal motive for oppression is the eagerness to pile up wealth, and this desire is connected with the fact that the oppressor is an idolater.

There is an almost complete absence of the theme of oppression in European and North American biblical theology. But the absence is not surprising, since it is possible to tackle this theme only within an existential situation of oppression.

Elsa Tamez,
Professor of Biblical Studies, Costa Rica

A sense of powerlessness lies at the root of poverty and hunger. We must stop confusing people by implying that more of the same – increased welfare spending alone, for example – will end poverty. Social welfare spending is absolutely necessary but it cannot address the needs of those who want to work. Instead we must strive to understand why people feel powerless and what it takes to address that powerlessness.

Frances Moore Lappe

> PSALM 72: 1-4
>
> *Give the king thy justice, O God, and thy righteousness to the royal son! May he judge thy people with righteousness, and thy poor with justice! Let the mountains bear prosperity for the people, and the hills, in righteousness! May he defend the cause of the poor of the people, give deliverance to the needy and crush the oppressor!*

REFLECTION • ACTION

1. Read the newspaper for a week with an eye toward how the media suggests where the blame rests. What analysis do you see taking place? Listen to Public Radio. Do you hear a more objective analysis there?

2. Ask someone at work (or your church) why they think there is so much hunger in the world. What do you think contributed to their analysis?

3. Take one issue of social injustice and plan to probe deeper into analysis for a period of time. Pray for guidance. Share with others what you discover. Look at who makes the decisions and who benefits from those decisions in the long run.

4. Read *Grace at the Table*, Enduring Hunger in God's World by David Beckmann and Arthur Simon, Intervarsity Press, 1999; and/or *The Powers That Be* by Walter Wink, Galilee Doubleday, 1998; and/or *Bible of the Oppressed* by Elsa Tamez, Orbis, 1982; and/or *How the Other Half Dies* by Susan George, Allanheld, Osmun & Co., 1977.

Pontius' Puddle

FROM CARING FOR HUMANS TO CARING FOR CREATION

> *The care of the earth is our most ancient and most worthy, and after all, our most pleasing responsibility. To cherish what remains of it and to foster its renewal is our only legitimate hope.*
>
> Wendell Berry, farmer and poet
> *The Unsettling of America*

The alarm needs to go off. Danger is ahead. We are on a collision course. Everywhere you look in the present state of the environment you see red warning lights. The major economic systems of the world and the care of the natural world are at odds. The survival of the earth is at stake. Thomas Berry, author of *The Dream of the Earth*, says "we are presently passing over one of the most significant thresholds in the entire course of history. Worldwide hunger is a scandal but social poverty is less devastating in the long haul than irreversible ecological poverty." Berry says that ecological refugees will soon be more numerous than political refugees.

What is the issue? Is it really that serious? Who is pushing the alarm button? Why haven't we been more informed? Will solutions affect my income? My security? How is the environment issue connected to other critical issues we face? Since we don't feel the effects yet can't we leave this for future generations? Maybe they are exaggerating. Won't technology and science find a solution? Isn't the church's main mission spiritual rather than material? Doesn't the *Bible* say the earth will pass away anyway, or will melt in the last judgment?

These and many other questions arise when the environment crisis is raised and action is needed. While there are some hopeful signs of progress and awareness, the big challenge before us is to sensitize people to the seriousness of the issue, begin to realize how the Christian attitude toward "dominion over the earth" has contributed to the problem, and begin to see that care of creation is also a mission of the Christian community. Ecology and faith are connected.

A disturbing factor is that the awareness of the crisis on the part of some (including the government) goes back many years. We have been warned. But for some reason the public in general and the church in particular has not taken it seriously. We have left the problem to the experts. Back in 1980 President Carter commissioned a study of the environmental crisis. Gerald Barney and Associates came up with an eight hundred page study called *The Global 2000 Report to the President*. It presented grim warnings and said that unless nations collectively take some hard steps, the world can expect a troubled entry into the twenty-first century. So now we are entering this century with the creation more threatened than ever in its history. Why has it become worse even after the warnings?

Thomas Berry says "If the earth does grow inhospitable to human presence, it is primarily because we have lost our sense of courtesy toward the earth and its inhabitants, our sense of gratitude, our willingness to recognize the sacred character of habitat, our capacity for the awesome, for the numinous quality of every earthly reality." (*Dream of the Earth*, p.2)

Some of the issues that threaten God's created order are:

• Toxic waste disposal	• Pollution of the seas and fresh water
• Global deforestation	• Destruction of the ozone shield
• Acid rain	• Pesticide and herbicide poisoning
• Salinization	• Green-house build up and global warming
• Water table depletion	• Economics without ecological ethics
• Topsoil erosion	• Little cooperation between nations
• Fossil fuel exhaustion	• Anthropocentric attitudes and action
• Over fishing	• Endangered species, both plant and animal
• Loss of bio-diversity	• Density of population
• Ignorance and apathy	• Radiation poisoning and nuclear proliferation

There are a number of good resources that can alert us to the nature of the crisis (see book list page 71. The media is beginning to become more responsible and honest. The church is calling us to return to the biblical mandate to care for God's creation, and enter into a relationship with nature where God's presence is revealed. Care of creation is more clearly connected to the problem of poverty and global economics by alert pastors.

Larry L. Rasmussen has written an excellent book that both presents the crisis in terms we can relate to, and gives us hope in our desire to take care of creation as followers of Jesus Christ. In his book *Earth Community – Earth Ethics*, Rasmussen reminds us that we belong to both the Christian community and nature's community. Both communities call for partnerships and stewardship. But our anthropocentrism has blinded us to the full reality. He lists some of the assumptions and values that have led the church and society to care for ourselves as humans at the expense of care for creation. A few examples are:

- Nature has a virtually limitless storehouse of resources for human use.

- Humanity has the commission to use and control nature.

- Humanity has the right to use nature's resources for an ongoing improvement of personal living.

- The quality of life itself is furthered by an economic system directed to ever-expanding material abundance.

- Modern science and technology have helped achieve a superior civilization in the West.

- The things we create are under our control.

- The good life is one of productive labor and material well-being.

An attitude needing change is to move beyond a human-centered focus to a creation-centered mission of caring for both the human community and nature's community. This will include a review of our present economic growth patterns and their effect on culture. Wes Jackson, founder of the Land Institute in Salem, Kansas reminds us that the same economic forces that destroy rainforests also destroy culture. Jackson suggests that cultural affirmation of the science/technology alignment with government and economic growth has been more ecologically destructive than the church/state alliance ever was. What is needed is a major shift in consciousness. The established cultural affirmations that see profit and growth as the bottom line will be just as resistant to this shift as the Catholic Church was to

Copernicus and Galileo. Jackson says, "too much was on the line for those church leaders to take a look through Galileo's telescope, but no more than when communities are being destroyed in our time while the dominant scientific technological establishment insists on the righteousness of its own theology." (*Becoming Native to This Place*)

Dean Freudenberger was my mentor when I first became conscientized about the environmental crisis. He has taught at both Methodist and Lutheran seminaries and is an author and popular speaker on the subject. In a speech he gave at a Caring for Creation Conference in Orange County, California in 1995, titled The Role of Faith Communities in Addressing the Environmental Crisis of the Twenty-first Century, he said, "In conclusion, caring for creation is the only tangible way that we can express our gratitude for our moment in the history of the earth. Caring for creation, for each other, and for the many generations yet to come is what makes us human. Caring about the environment crisis and working for a sustainable and therefore just future for all life, be it human, or non-human life, transcends the more simplistic motivation of enlightened self interest. We are motivated not by fear, but by love. Faith gives us the possibility of attempting and accomplishing the things which seem impossible."

John Cobb, Jr., co-author with Herman Daly of *For the Common Good*, has been a long-time advocate of a better balance of Christianity, economics and ecology. In a presentation he made at Harvard University in 1998 he outlined some principles for structuring a responsible economic order on the part of faith communities. He said the church needs to repent of its neglect to care about the earth and be ready to make sacrifices. Cobb said, "We need to renew our commitment to help shape social, environmental, economic and technological policies and hold our government leaders accountable. People of faith need to overcome their reticence to examine current assumptions of the experts and engage in dialogue with them. We must stress the importance of the study of the scriptures, theology and ethics with a strong commitment to education at all levels about the eco-justice crisis. More concerned people can practice the three R's of reducing, reusing and recycling. The church must also work for new forms of governance that will safeguard the health of communities of life and their future."

OTHER VOICES

Technology and Care of the Earth

The two worlds of biosphere and techno-sphere are out of balance, indeed potentially in deep conflict. Humans are in the middle. Too often we have given the green light to new technology without asking the hard ethical questions. It is a critical moment. We stand at the door of the future opening onto a crisis more sudden, more global, more inescapable and more bewildering than any ever encountered by the human species, and one that will take decisive shape within the life-span of children who are already born.

Barbara Ward and Rene Dubos

Ethics of Compassion and Responsibility

What we need today is not a new morality but a new ethics; that is, attentiveness to change and the ability to adapt to what must be done at each moment – and today that means protecting the planet and all its systems, defending and promoting life, starting with those that are most threatened. Two principles embody this ethics: the responsibility principle, and the compassion principle.

Leonardo Boff, Liberation theologian and author of:
Cry of the Earth, Cry of the Poor

The earth which nourishes me has a rightful claim upon my work and energy in return. I have no right to despise the earth on which I live and move. I am bound to it by loyalty and gratitude. It is as a guest and a pilgrim that God has called me into this pilgrimage. It would be evading God's call if I were to dream away my earthly life in longing thoughts of heaven. There is such a thing as an impious longing for the world to come; its hope is in vain.

Dietrich Bonhoeffer

> 2 Chronicles 7:14
>
> *If my people who are called by name will humble themselves, pray, seek my face and turn from their wicked ways, then will I hear from heaven, and will forgive their sin and* **heal their land.**

Job 12:7-10

But ask the animals and they will teach you;
the birds of the air, and they will tell you,
ask the plants of the earth and they will teach you;
and the fish of the sea will declare to you
who among all these does not know
that the hand of the Lord has done this?
In God's hand is the life of every loving thing
and the breath of every human being.

REFLECTION • ACTION

1. What or who has helped you to become more aware of our relationship to the earth and its environment? What has kept you from being more alert about the current ecological crisis? Find a way to be in better communication with nature's community. What difference does it make when I see myself as a guest on the earth?

2. What are some signs of environmental degradation and suffering that you see in your community, your society, and your workplace? What is being done to make people aware and bring about change? Be alert to what political campaigns are saying about action needed to preserve and protect our environment.

3. In what ways do economic systems and values affect our care of creation? Listen or look carefully for current news items that lift up the environmental crisis. Encourage your pastor to make care of creation part of the church's mission and message, even the Sunday liturgy and prayers.

4. Read *Earth Community-Earth Ethics* by Larry L. Rasmussen, Orbis Books, 1996; and/or *Patching God's Garment,* Environment and Mission in the Twenty-first Century by W. Dayton Roberts, MARC World Vision, 1994; and/or *The Dream of the Earth* by Thomas Berry, Sierra Club, 1988; and/or *Theology of the Land*, edited by Bernard Evans and Gregory Cusack, The Liturgical Press, 1987.

FEELINGS AND FRUSTRATION

WHY ARE THEY GROWING SUGAR (CASH CROPS) INSTEAD OF FOOD CROPS...WHO DECIDES?

FROM ANSWERS TO QUESTIONS

> *Faith that does not doubt is dead faith.*
>
> Miguel de Unamuno
>
> *A man living on the edge between faith and doubt wrote to me, "I've always felt drawn to God and to the hope that life has meaning. Often I struggle with, for want of a better word, nihilism. There is so much suffering and evil in this world. Belief in a good God is not an easy thing for anyone who 'thinks' to any significant degree." It's that kind of doubting faith — or faithful doubting — with which I've wanted to dialogue in this book. I think I understand it. It's where I live too, most of the time.*
>
> Douglas John Hall; Preface, *Why Christian?*

I went to hear Murray Haar, a college professor from Augustana College (Sioux Falls) speak on the topic of social ethics and the church. Dr. Haar is a seminary graduate and professor of religion, a Christian Jew, whose father was in Aushwitz during the Holocaust. His speech took me by surprise. I wasn't ready for some of the things he said. He left me with more questions than answers. His questions, however, brought me closer to understanding God's call than any set of easy answers.

Haar told us that when he was a child he remembers how his father met him after school each day and asked him, "Did you ask a good question today?" He never asked him what he had learned at school, but what questions he had asked. From his father he learned that questions are holy. Preachers today, Haar said, give too many answers and do not help people ask the right questions. He encouraged us to end some of our sermons with a question. "Send the people home with a question," he said. "This may give more hope and bring people closer to the kingdom of God."

"Certain questions," said Tolstoy, "are put to humankind not that we should answer them, but that we should ever wrestle with them." William Sloan Coffin, Jr. said in a sermon at Riverside Church in New York City, "The travesty of higher education is that it spends most of its time training its students to answer unimportant answerable questions."

The biblical message from beginning to end is filled with questions; "Where are you?" was God's first question in Genesis and then, "Where is your brother?" The prophets used the question to help people examine their lives and listen to God. Isaiah asked, "Why do you spend money for that which is not bread, and labor for that which does not satisfy?" (55:2). Then, in chapter fifty-eight the prophet speaking for God raises the question about their ritual of fasting. It had become a mere formality and did not involve them in the struggle for justice: "Will you call this a fast?" God asks. This opens the door for Isaiah to proclaim a true fast, which includes feeding the hungry and correcting oppression.

The psalmist is not afraid to question God. Questions seem to serve as part of the healing process: "My God, my God, why have you forsaken me?" (Psalm 22). In Malachi the prophet asks a question to provoke the covenant people to remember the covenant: "Will any rob God?" he asks, "yet you are robbing me, says the Lord!" They did not think that withholding the tithe was stealing from God. The question, not the answer was a way to awaken the conscience.

Jesus was an artist at asking questions to get across his message. William Herzog II demonstrates this in his book *Jesus, Justice and the Reign of God* in chapter seven when he calls attention to Jesus' question: What is written? How do you read? Ernest Campbell, an eloquent Presbyterian preacher, developed a series of seven sermons as part of his Lenten Sunday preaching (not a bad idea) on questions Jesus asked. Each question opened the door to proclamation of both judgment and grace, the cross and resurrection

> *"What did you go out to see?"* Expectations determine perceptions.
> *"What is the Kingdom of God?"* The kingdom, Jesus' main theme.
> *"Who made me judge over you?"* A reprimand before the lesson.
> *"Do you think I have come to give peace?"* When justice meets resistance.
> *"Who do you say that I am?"* Getting beyond creed and statements.
> *"Have you come out against a robber?"* God's leverage is love, not violence.
> *"Why do you weep?"* Our search for significance.

When it comes to our response to human suffering, pain and oppression, we must ask some important questions. Jim Wallis, in his new book *Faith Works*, tells how questions led him on a journey of faith and action for poor people. He warns that questions can be dangerous and can cause discomfort among the privileged. Dom Helder Camara, who served as a bishop in Brazil for many years, did a wonderful job in raising the consciousness of people in his country. He made a statement which reminds us that raising the question may get us in trouble. Camara once said, "When I help feed the hungry they call me a saint. When I teach the hungry to read and to vote and to question their circumstances of poverty, I am a troublemaker and a communist."

Frances Moore Lappe, co-author with Joseph Collins of *Food First,* joined others who were interested in the hunger and food issues in the early 1970s. She became suspicious of the answers to the food crisis being given by government agencies and corporate America. To get beyond popular myths about the causes of hunger, she began to ask some questions that provoked, awakened and changed the direction of many efforts to address the hunger crises.

After attending the World Food Conference in 1974 Lappe became convinced that the so-called experts didn't have the answers that would solve the food problem. They weren't asking the right questions, such as: What economic decisions result in hunger? Who has control over decisions that are supposed to help the hungry? What releases human ingenuity and energy that can help bring about changes that are needed? What values contribute to aid policies of government and non-government agencies? How can hungry people become our allies rather than dependants? How can they become more involved in analysis and development projects? Lappes first book *Diet For a Small Planet* raised important questions.

In a speech Lappe gave to a large ecumenical gathering at the church I served in Long Beach, California, she reminded us that the answers for the world food problems are larger than our span of life. If we expect to see the answers in our lifetime we have not asked big enough questions. She then quoted someone who said, "Nothing worth doing is completed in one's lifetime. So we live by hope." She wasn't quoting Jesus but it did sound like her thinking was influenced by his teaching.

OTHER VOICES

Follow your heart, trust your questions and pursue them until you find answers that satisfy you. How questions get into our heads and souls is a great mystery...These questions of the heart, as I like to call them, are an entry-way into our spirituality. They beckon us to a deeper place and a more honest life; they are a call to conscience and, ultimately, an invitation to transformation...The most important thing is that the questions be diligently followed; to turn away from them is to turn away from the voice of your own conscience, and, perhaps, the voice of God.

Jim Wallis, *Faith Works*

Rarely do we find people who willingly engage in hard, solid thinking. There is an almost universal quest for easy answers and half-baked solutions. Nothing pains some people more than having to think.

Martin Luther King, Jr., Baptist Pastor

Loving God with Our Mind and Heart

When all is said and done, I write out of my faith commitment as a Christian and not in an attempt to create controversy. But where this faith has been corrupted into literalized propositional statements, I have become its exposer and its critic. I have come to see the controversy that ensues not as negative and not ever as destructive to the church. I regard it rather as a positive sign of health and vitality. It reveals the willingness to explore the truth of God without seeking to protect God from the disturbance of new insights. It arises out of the sense that God must be worshiped with the mind as well as the heart.

John Shelby Spong, Episcopal Bishop

JOHN 9:1-3

As he was walking along he saw a man blind from birth. His disciples asked him, "Rabbi, who sinned, this man or his parents, that he was born blind?" Jesus answered, "neither this man or his parents sinned; he was born blind so that God's works might be revealed in him."

> JOHN 6:66-68
>
> *Because of this many of his disciples turned back and no longer went about with him. So Jesus asked the twelve, "Do you wish to go away?" Simon Peter answered him, "Lord, to whom can we go? You have the words of eternal life."*

REFLECTION • ACTION

1. What question still bugs you? What happens if we wait until we have all the answers before we act on behalf of others who suffer injustice?

2. How have questions or a question helped you to understand, become awakened, or take a different path in your faith journey? Must there be a right answer to every question?

3. Think of a question that would be good to ask a candidate for public office that would be helpful in learning if this person understands why there is hunger and poverty in the world. Find a way to ask the question. How does asking why people are hungry sometimes change the direction of the conversation or the response?

4. Read *Why Christian?* by Douglas John Hall, Fortress Press 1998; and/or *Mañana* by Justo L. Gonzales, Abington 1990; and/or *The God We Never Knew* by Marcus Borg, Harper Collins 1997; and/or *Do You Love Me? Jesus Questions the Church* by Michael Crosby, Orbis, 2000; and/or *Becoming a Thinking Christian* by John B. Cobb Jr., Abingdon, 1993.

Pontius' Puddle

77

FROM WEALTH TO PARTNERSHIP

> *Tell me then, whence thou art rich? The root and origin of it must have been injustice. Why? Because God in the beginning made not one man rich, and another poor. Nor did God afterward take and show to one treasures of gold, and deny to the other the right of searching for it; but God left the earth free to all alike. Why then, if it is common, have you so many areas of land, while your neighbor has not a portion of it?*
>
> John Chrysostom
> *Great Preacher of the Fourth Century*

The issues related to the pain and suffering of so many people in the world are multiple, complex and interconnected. It matters not where you start or which issue you tackle, your journey in loving your neighbor will always take you into the economic arena. There is no way around it. It is impossible to follow Jesus in showing compassion to the poor and oppressed without facing the issue of wealth (money), its origin, its significance and its connection to the Kingdom of God. We all need to deal with it.

So why not think about it, teach about it and find ways to be more honest and open in our efforts to move beyond guilt, powerlessness and fear? Too long have we been reluctant or afraid to bring economics into the discussion of what it means to be a Christian. Too long have we allowed modern exegetes (interpreters of scripture) to ignore what the *Bible* says about greed, wealth and its relation to poverty and exploitation. Too long have we allowed culture to dictate for us what are the acceptable values that relate to possessions, profit and poverty. Too long have we been so preoccupied with pure doctrine and church structures, that there is little energy or attention given to the scandal of economic injustice and the danger of differentiating wealth. Too long have we tranquilized our conscience by allowing the corporate world to be greedy for us without questioning the origins of wealth and economic growth.

Where do we begin? One can begin with the scriptures. But we must remember that we always bring with us to the scriptures our own situation in life, our attitudes, our experiences and our traditions. So why not begin with the context of the world we live in and the history of where we have come from? It will make a difference in the questions we ask as we study the *Bible*. The book of Acts reveals that the early Christian communities didn't start with a Book of Order or Small Catechism. Their memory of Jesus, their experiences of God's presence and action in their lives helped them know what to believe and what to do. The context influenced their perceptions and proclamation. The search for an answer to "who is Jesus?" must involve an awareness of the events and crises of his day.

Any reading of the present context of the world we live in will reveal a great chasm between the rich and the poor. All indications suggest that the chasm is getting wider. Most of us are better off financially while the scandal of poverty continues to grow and threaten our survival. Richard Foster begins his book *Freedom of Simplicity* by saying, "Contemporary culture is plagued by the passion to possess," and suggests that there is no escape from the trap of "more is better." We moved into the twenty-first century heralding the great economic growth in the United States. In 1999 there were eight million more millionaires than the year before. Is that good news? For whom is that good news? At what cost?

Some economists are daring to challenge the dominant view. George Soros, philanthropist, economist and one of the world's richest persons, was born in Budapest. He made a billion dollars betting against the British pound and later lost two billion dollars in Russia. Soros knows capitalism intimately and is not optimistic about what he sees, blaming what he calls 'market fundamentalism' for reducing hunger and social relations to the common denominator of money. Soros argues that unregulated markets when left alone, ignore common interests in favor of individual self interest. He is an advocate of a more global system of political decision making to help regulate a truly global economy. For more information on this see his book *The Crisis of Global Capitalism*.

Most of us are wealthy. Maybe we are not millionaires, but by comparison to most of the world, we are financially wealthy. Does God want us to feel guilty about that? Is wealth itself a bad thing? What does the *Bible* say? Jose

Miranda, a Mexican theologian, has a very thorough study of the biblical view of wealth in his book *Communism in the Bible*. I'm sure it is out of print now. He points out several things that most of us miss in our study of wealth in the *Bible*. Miranda begins by reminding us that, "Jesus has no horror of wealth, neither in itself nor in its use and enjoyment. What Jesus condemns is differentiating or relative wealth, wealth in the midst of poverty." The story of the rich man and Lazarus is a case in point. What is punished in hell says Miranda is that some are rich and others are poor. He goes on to point out the connection between injustice and wealth, that most wealth is acquired at the expense of others who are exploited. We may argue with that but then arguing with the *Bible* is allowed in our search for the truth. Our greater sin is to ignore it.

Jeremiah struggles with the rich getting richer and the poor getting poorer. He calls our attention to the connection between riches and poverty:

> *Like cages filled with birds, so are their houses full of what they have taken by fraud: This is how they have become great and rich. Fat and slack they have grown; they went beyond the words of evil: they did no justice, they trod upon the rights of orphans, they respected not the justice of the poor.* Jeremiah 5:27-28

If we were to ask about Jesus' attitude toward wealth, where would it take us? No one would argue that he gave serious warnings about it. "Be aware of covetousness," he said. He saw wealth as a serious danger because it has a way of blinding, cursing and dividing people. Many of his parables are given with a keen awareness of the economic situation of his day. A more careful reading of them will show how they are intended to challenge current systems that keep some people poor. See William Herzog's *The Parables as Subversive Speech*.

Another interesting study is the history of preaching by the early Christians regarding the origin, significance and use of wealth. Justo Gonzalez, a Methodist church historian, has done a convincing and thorough study of this (*Faith and Wealth*). He concludes that the subject was a dominant theme in the preaching of our apostolic fathers. One wonders why those who lived much closer to the time Jesus lived in Palestine made economics part of their proclamation, while today it is seldom part of preaching about Jesus. It was not just the well being of the poor that was their concern but the salvation of the rich. A strange silence about the relationship of discipleship to economics took place when Christianity became the state religion under Constantine in the fourth century. Church leaders wanted to continue their position of privilege with the government.

How can we move beyond the fact that many of us have acquired considerable wealth? How can wealthy Christians respond to the call of God in their lives? One way is to move in the direction of partnership, engaging in a kind of solidarity with those who are poor and oppressed.

Organizations like Ministry of Money and Journey Into Freedom sponsor trips to various parts of the world where poverty is rampant. Exposure to the realities of poor people is often a good place to start toward partnership. It can radically change one's perspective and priorities while moving beyond guilt, powerlessness and fear.

Partnership means an attitude toward one's possessions that acknowledges God's ownership of all things. It is not my wealth. It is God's wealth. The early church saw their possessions as common. When anyone had a need, they were attended to by the community. Partnership places a strong value on Christian community. It is sometimes called solidarity.

Partnership also means a willingness to address the causes that keep some living in poverty. For example, it means working with various organizations to bring about debt relief of poor nations so that millions of God's creatures might live. In Ron Sider's book *Rich Christians in an Age of Hunger,* he points out that the neglect of the biblical teaching on structural injustice is one of the most deadly omissions of evangelicalism today. Partnership includes responsible stewardship of our finances, citizenship and relationships. In giving money to help end hunger and poverty Sider suggests that twenty percent be given for emergency relief, forty percent for development programs, twenty percent to heighten awareness and change lifestyles, and twenty percent for advocacy to bring about change in public policy. In Sider's new book *Just Generosity* he includes a pledge that he encourages Christians to consider.

GENEROUS CHRISTIAN'S PLEDGE

I pledge to open my heart to God's call to care as much about the poor as the *Bible* does. I therefore commit:

- *Daily,* to pray for the poor, beginning with the Generous Christian Prayer: Lord Jesus, teach my heart to share your love for the poor.

- *Weekly,* to minister at least one hour, helping, serving, sharing with and mostly getting to know someone in need.

- *Monthly,* to study at least one story, book, article or film about the plight of the poor and hungry and discuss it with others.

- *Yearly,* to retreat for a few hours to meditate on this one question in the light of scripture: "Is caring for the poor as important in my life at it is in the *Bible?*" and to examine my budget and priorities in light of it, asking God what changes he/she would like me to make in the use of my time, money, influence and citizenship.

Sider encourages those who commit to this pledge to find a small group where they can find encouragement and support in being accountable to their pledge.

Isaiah 65:19-23

I will rejoice in Jerusalem, and delight in my people; no more shall the sound of weeping be heard in it, or the cry of distress. No more shall there be in it an infant that lives but a few days, or an old person who does not live out a lifetime. They shall build houses and inhabit them; they shall plant vineyards and eat their fruit. They shall not build and another inhabit; they shall not plant and another eat... my chosen shall long enjoy the work of their hands. They shall not labor in vain.

Matthew 6:19-21

Do not store up for yourselves treasures on earth where moth and rust consume and where thieves break in and steal. But store up for yourselves treasure in heaven...for where your treasure is there will your heart be also.

REFLECTION • ACTION

1. What are some popular attitudes toward wealth that one must challenge in order to follow the teachings of Jesus? Someone said "It is a sin to die rich. Get rid of it all before you die." Think about this and its ramifications for a better world.

2. Discuss the Generous Christians Pledge above. What do you like about it? What would be most difficult? What is new about it compared to your current response?

3. How has your worshipping community or church dealt with the issue of wealth and economic injustice? What would be helpful to you? Who should you talk to?

4. What is socially responsible investing? What is the screening process needed if we want our investments to be used to create a better world? Why not check your investment portfolio periodically in light of God's concern for the weak and vulnerable. Attend a Ministry of Money retreat. Call 301-428-9560.

5. Read *Virtue and Affluence* – the Challenge of Wealth by John C. Haughey, Sheed L. Ward, 1997; and/or *The Crisis in the Churches* by Robert Wuthnow, Oxford University Press, 1997; and/or *Faith and Wealth*: Early Christian Ideas on the Origin, Significance and Use of Money by Justo Gonzalez, Harper and Row, 1990; and/or *The Crisis of Global Capitalism* by George Soros, Public Affairs, 1998.

FROM DESPAIR TO HOPE

> *We must become good plowmen. Hope is the prerequisite of plowing. What sort of farmer plows the furrow in the autumn but has no hope for the spring? So, too, we accomplish nothing without hope, without a sure inner hope that a new age is about to dawn. Hope is strength. The energy in the world is equal to the hope in it. And even if only a few people share such hope, a power is created which nothing can hold down – it inevitably spreads to others.*
>
> Albert Schweitzer

How do you keep going when everything seems hopeless? Where do you turn to find courage, energy, or motivation to hang in there when you have every reason to quit? What can you do about feelings of fear, apathy, despair and cynicism especially when it seems that you are all alone in the struggle? How does one handle compassion fatigue?

These are questions asked not only by those who are experiencing death and destruction firsthand. They are questions many of us ask who live in affluence and among the oppressors. They are questions raised by people who have joined forces with those who work to change the systems that perpetuate oppression, racism and other forms of human suffering. Almost everyone who enters the struggle will, at one time or another, experience frustration, despair and aloneness.

We can identify with the Israelite living in exile who said, "How shall we sing the Lord's song in a strange (hostile) land?" (Psalm 137:4) It is a question asked by millions who find themselves exiles in their own country, among their traditional and familiar people and churches. How can we sing of deliverance when every day more of us are imprisoned? When, no matter who is in office, things don't seem to change?

Hope often is considered subversive by the keepers of the status quo because it refuses to give up, to believe that things cannot change. Prophets often are silenced or killed because they build a vision of a different world and thereby keep hope alive. Managers of the status quo are enemies of hope. Every center of power in an evil world fears the poet, prophet and artist because they communicate hope and imagination.

In order to move beyond guilt and powerlessness we must remain hopeful. Yes, faith, hope and love abide (I Corinthians 13:13). Because Paul says the greatest of these is love does not negate the importance of hope in our lives. In speaking to various groups about social justice issues I have described hope in these ways:

- Hope is found in the willingness to embrace pain and to express it.
- Hope is the willingness to act before all the evidence is in, not being afraid to risk.
- Hope is rooted in community and grows as we are present to one another.
- Hope is balancing a sense of urgency with humor and playfulness.
- Hope is remembering that God is in charge and we are not the Messiah.
- Hope is found in remaining close to nature and celebrating God's creation.
- Hope is nurtured through music and the arts.

Hope emerges out of the ashes of our dreams because God brings life out of death. What we see is a valley of dry bones, but our new eyesight enables us to see those bones come alive with flesh. The hope of God's people is renewed through the promise of our baptism. It is God's presence we celebrate at the eucharistic meal, and as a result we are energized. As a friend said, "Our hope is deathly foolish, like the cross of Christ." But our foolish hope keeps faith alive and rekindles the fire of love within our hearts. It is this hope that keeps us working toward and expecting the reign of God. It may sound crazy but hope helps us to pray with confidence: "Thy kingdom come, thy will be done on earth."

OTHER VOICES

From *The City of Joy*
Calcutta, India

The compound was first and foremost the children's domain. "Marvelous children of the city of Joy," Kovalski would say. Little innocent beings nourished on poverty, from whom the life force never ceased to burst forth. Their freedom from care, their zest for life, their magical smiles and dark faces set off by luminous gazes colored the entire world in which they lived with beauty. If the adults here managed to retain some spark of hope, was it not because of them, because of their dazzling freshness, because of the earnestness of their games? Without them the slums would have been nothing but prisons. It was they who managed to turn these places of distress into places of Joy.

Dominique La Pierre

For those who believe in Christ, there is no sorrow that is not mixed with hope – no despair. There is only a constant being born again; a constantly going from darkness to light.

Vincent Van Gogh

THE POOR ARE THE TEACHERS

The vicar general of the San Salvador archdiocese says to us, "It is the poor who evangelize us and preach to us. Often when one feels depressed and just spends a little time with the poor – you cannot imagine how much it changes a person. Three years ago a woman came to me whose daughter and niece had been dragged away.

"A day later she found both corpses; the heads had been cut off. I didn't know how I should comfort her; my voice failed me, but she began to comfort me.She said to me, 'Monsignor, I simply opened my Bible, I read Psalm 92, and I felt comforted.' I looked up the Psalm when I got home, and for the first time I understood it. God is the only savior. That gives us hope: a people that has faith, not this passive faith, but active. In the church today we need a real conversion."

Dorothee Soelle,
from *Theology for Skeptics*

1 PETER 1:3

Blessed be the God and Father of our Lord Jesus Christ! By his great mercy we have been born anew to a living hope through the resurrection of Jesus Christ from the dead.

EXODUS 3:7-8

Then the Lord said, "I have seen the affliction of my people who are in Egypt, and have heard their cry because of their taskmasters; I know their sufferings, and I have come down to deliver them out of the hand of the Egyptians, and to bring them up out of that land to a good and broad land, a land flowing with milk and honey."

REFLECTION • ACTION

1. It has been said that people are changed more by exciting their imagination than by reminding them of what is right and wrong. What do you think about this? Give an example.

2. We keep hope alive by telling the story over and over again. That's why we keep coming back to worship Sunday after Sunday. Find a story of hope in this book and tell it to someone you know who may need a word of hope.

3. In what way can hope be considered subversive? To whom is it subversive? Who stands to lose today if hope for change is kept alive? What sign of hope have you witnessed recently, or read about?

4. Read *Good News About Injustice, A Witness of Courage in a Hurting World* by Gary A. Haugen, InterVarsity Press, 1999; and/or *Prophetic Imagination*, by Walter Brueggemann, Fortress, 1978, and/or *We Drink From Our Own Wells* by Gustavo Guitierrez, Orbis/Dove, 1984; and/or *City of Joy* by Dominique La Pierre, Warner Books, 1986; and/or *Jesus: A New Vision* by Marcus Borg, Harper, 1987.

FROM CERTAINTY TO AMBIGUITY

> When I moved to Latin America I was teaching spirituality and prayer. I had it together on that level and I decided to stay out of anything close to politics or economics. But gradually I realized that I couldn't avoid the political, economic and military...mess that is there to be seen. Suddenly I had this image that indeed Christ himself was called political, subversive, and was crucified as a competitor of the worldly king. I remembered that Judas was interested in money, and that money had a lot to do with the suffering of Christ. I realized that there were soldiers and military people all around the Lord, who came to his crucifixion. I saw then that our spiritual call takes place in the midst of ambiguity and ambivalence and that if I waited until I had a very clear, final view of how things really were before I started saying anything, I would never speak. So here I am, a little bit unclear, a little nervous, saying things that I am not competent in, but claiming the competence of the Christian to speak clearly and specifically in a time of crisis.
>
> Henri Nouwen
> from *Gracias*

Most of us are more comfortable with solutions than with questions. We prefer closures rather than paradox. There is security with certainty. When faced with a problem we generally approach it with the assumption that information, insight and proper action will bring satisfactory solutions. We want to fix things right now. In a success-oriented culture, living with ambiguity is not a sign of stability or progress.

However, the reality of a broken world and the variety of analyses of root causes often lead to ambiguity rather than certainty. What we thought, believed, assumed, or followed is suddenly brought into question. It isn't as clear-cut and simple as we were led to believe. Sometimes long-held assumptions are discovered to be inadequate if not false! Receiving more information unsettles us rather than making things clear and easy. Digging deeper only muddies the water.

There usually are two sides to an argument. Listening to the other side is important even though it may be painful. Living, as we do, in a world where everything tends to be labeled right or wrong, we may tend to shy away from ambiguity. Action that is both good and bad is difficult to accept. So people eagerly listen to those who have the easy answers and can assuredly distinguish between the right way and the wrong way.

Ambiguity also is found within us. Part of me wants to lay down my life for those who suffer. Part of me doesn't. Sometimes I may be enthusiastic, energetic and highly motivated. Within a short time I may feel quite different and wonder why. Which person is the real me? Paul shares this ambiguity in Romans 7 (see page 91).

Wholeness and healing involve pain. Sometimes that includes the pain of ambiguity or the pain of having to change one's previous position. It should not surprise us that our journey into the lives of those who cry for help will be discomforting. We will go back and forth in our analysis and conclusions. In that process it is important to be centered in the gospel, the good news that God accepts us, understands us and forgives us. It also is important to remember that Jesus' compassion for the poor and the biblical commitment to justice and righteousness is not ambiguous. This can hold us on course as we struggle through the mixed messages we hear and the ambiguous feelings we experience.

OTHER VOICES

Journal Keeping in Honduras

Being here, I think, is like watching a terrifying movie. I have seen hideous, nauseating poverty, heard horrifying tales of death, and seen fear trembling across faces. I have met thin and anxious men and women just returned from working in refugee camps who have driven, afraid for their lives, through war on the borders. Honduras shares its borders with El Salvador to the west and Nicaragua to the south. At the United States embassy in

Tegucigalpa, I have heard information officers explain our military presence in Central America as "a good thing." From Hondurans I have heard opposition to that presence. My life back home is slow, orderly and without drama. This trip, like a movie, is fast, and it keeps breaking with life-and-death events. I am weary, hot, confused. It has begun to dawn on me, in me, not as fact but with wrenching feeling, that the lives here are connected to my life.

Our short stay in Honduras provides us with conflicting views: the official U.S. position, and that of Hondurans and international relief workers who oppose our nation's policies. Most of the members of our group feel great anguish in muggy Tegucigalpa. We are intelligent, educated church goers–"solid American citizens." No matter with whom we agree, we are discomfited.

One man in our group, after 10 years service as a soldier on active duty and as a reservist, felt persuaded by what he saw and heard in Honduras to resign his captaincy in the U.S. Army. "I cried for my country in Tegucigalpa," he wrote later in his hometown paper. "I wept for the hurt and turmoil my country is creating for millions of Latin Americans...I saw American soldiers being used as an instrument of a foreign policy which says, 'If it isn't in the U. S. model, then it is wrong.' " And whether we agreed or disagreed with this young man, that morning in the lobby of our hotel in Tegucigalpa, when he told us his decision, we wept with him.

But I will speak, now, only for myself. At this point what seems most important for the 20 of us from 12 states is not that we have learned who is "right" and who is "wrong." We have not. We never will. Few of us will ever even know "what to do." But our sense of the human family has been unalterably enlarged. We have seen, many of us for the first time, what hunger, war, hopelessness and fear can do. In our own daily, humdrum lives, it will be difficult to forget the faces, voices, smells, homes of the countries we visited. We have also seen signs of hope. Adela and her Base Christian Communities, Dona Heyde in her CODE offices, the Nicaraguan barrios, schools, factories being rebuilt and people hoping. When we repeat the Lord's Prayer, the names of the "our," whose Father he is, have increased. And when we listen for an answer, we may recall Dona Heyde's statement, that hot afternoon in Tegucigalpa: "God speaks in the voice of the people."

Judith Moore,
Journalist

ROMANS 7:15-21

I do not understand my own actions. For I do not do what I want, but I do the very thing I hate. Now if I do what I do not want, I agree that the law is good. So then it is no longer I that do it, but sin which dwells within me. For I know that nothing good dwells within me, that is, in my flesh. I can will what is right, but I cannot do it. For I do not do the good I want, but the evil I do not want is what I do. Now if I do what I do not want, it is no longer I that do it, but sin which dwells within me.

So I find it to be a law that when I want to do right, evil lies close at hand.

REFLECTION • ACTION

1. What questions still go unanswered for you regarding the role of a Christian in responding to poverty and oppression?

2. What has become more clear or less clear, as you have continued on in your Christian faith? As you have responded to the cries of oppression in the world?

3. Think of actions you have taken to alleviate human suffering, even though you didn't have total certainty on the issues. What might God be leading you to do next?

4. Read *The Window of Vulnerability,* a Political Spirituality by Dorothee Soelle, Fortress Press, 1990; and/or *Naked Before God,* The Return of a Broken Disciple by Bill Williams, Morehouse Publishing, 1998; and/or *The Paradox of Plenty* edited by Douglas Boucher, Food First Books, 1999.

FROM CONCERN TO OUTRAGE

> *Without anger change doesn't happen...Anger is the only thing that breaks people out of their chains.*
>
> Bill Williams

> *Our task is 'to refine the raw ore of emotion and transmute it into the pure metal of competent, systematic – and successful – action. Moral or religious indignation, however necessary, is not enough. Emotion by itself never made anything – no poems, no marriages, no justice. Yet without our untidy welter of love, generosity, anger, fear, outrage, we would never be motivated to change any thing; we would be prisoners of the status quo.*
>
> Susan George

There is something to be said for diplomacy and tact. We usually make more progress toward improving things by remaining cool, polite, balanced, reasonable and objective. Being diplomatic is an art we all need to learn and use with discretion.

But there is also something to be said for outrage. Anger is an emotion that can be used creatively for improving things. Jesus expressed strong emotion when he drove the money-changers out of the temple (John 2:13-22). The writers of the *Bible* are not hesitant to tell us about the anger of God and the wrath of God.

If we are made in the image of God, does this mean we too will be moved to the point of outrage when we witness the injustices done to God's children and the destruction of God's beautiful work of creation? Is it a perversion of love to think that love can be present within us without any sense of outrage toward injustice, in light of global reality today?

Robert McAfee Brown says we need moral outrage within the Christian community in order to bring about the justice of God in society. He claims that we need to recover some of the moral madness of the Old Testament prophets. But that's scary because we've seen how destructive anger can be. We also remember what happened to many of the prophets who spoke out.

Maybe a starting point is to accept the fact that anger is a human feeling that can be a way of moving us to action on behalf of others. Surprisingly, anger is not something foreign to compassion. Theologian Beverly Henderson reminds us that anger signals attention to our awareness that all is not right with the world, and as such can be an ally. She connects the power of anger to the work of love and the work of justice.

I am discovering more and more that if we are willing to learn what's happening to poor people today, as well as to learn the causes of poverty and oppression, if we are willing to get behind and beneath the explanations of poverty given by the beneficiaries from the present systems, we will become more outraged. And that outrage is a sign of the image of God within us. It is part of compassion.

Outrage energizes us for action. It takes us out of our lethargy and indifference. When we are outraged, we look for something to do rather than be content with what may seem hopeless. It takes a dose of outrage at injustice to find the courage to say no to the Caesars of our day who clamor for our allegiance and who want things to remain as they are.

OTHER VOICES

How Does One Handle the Rage in the Pit of One's Stomach?

For one hour I sat between two volunteer counselors at Black Sash in Johannesburg. I listened as Blacks told their stories of being cheated, exploited, deprived of livelihood, and trapped by unfair laws and regulations. All this was done legally under a system called apartheid. Inside I wanted to scream. How can some human beings do this to other humans? I had to leave before my anger became visible.

Driving through different countries in Africa, I saw fields of fertile land, rich with the capacity to feed everyone. And then I visited the peasants in their poor housing with no sanitation, no clean water and only enough food to survive if the rains continued.

Perhaps in my rage, in my urge to scream at God, God was screaming at me, at us and at our institutions and social systems that cause and perpetuate hunger and inequality.

I listened to development and government workers tell how aid is often determined not by need as much as by which government follows the directives of our government, or which project strengthens U.S. security and status in the world. Hearing and seeing this made me feel embarrassed, angry and guilty. Sometimes I cried. I wanted to step up to someone from among those affected by our corporate greed and blindness and say, "I'm really sorry for what we have allowed to happen. Please forgive us."

I asked one of our missionaries, "Do you ever get over the anger you feel when you see how Africans are treated by Whites (both African and non-African), how the poor are left so helpless in their poverty while others get richer?" He said, "No, not really. But you learn how to handle it." Another said, "When you do get over your anger, it's time to leave and go home."

While many of Africa's problems are imported from abroad, many others are not. The rage within was also felt while witnessing the results of senseless brutality and political exploitations by African leaders. One relief worker posed the question to me: "Starve the city dwellers and they riot. Starve the peasants and they die. If you were a politician, which would you choose?"

This feeling of rage in the pit of one's stomach has something to do with God. It is the presence of God in us that yearns for justice and hurts when injustice takes place. Pity may be void of anger but not compassion. Not until we allow the feeling of anger to surface as we see the injustice and needless suffering of people will we take the necessary action and be able to say, "In the name of Jesus, stand up and walk."

Dorothee Soelle reminds us that: "If we want to work for justice we must acquaint ourselves with the inner feeling of rage and anger over being too little, too weak, too few to prevent what is happening before our eyes. Too often this feeling has been dulled or somehow gets lost. But if you listen carefully you will discover a power within to allow this outrage to become redemptive."

From *Out of Africa* by George S. Johnson

Capacity for Outrage

Abraham Heschel never "lost the capacity for outrage." During the war years he spoke to a Stanford University ethics class. It turned out that a friend of one of the students, both of whom were Jewish, was producing napalm. The student asked Heschel what she should say to him. "Go to him," Heschel replied, with barely concealed trembling of limb, "and tell him that if he continues making napalm he forfeits the name of Jew. Go to him and tell him that if he continues to create such things he forfeits the name of human being. Go to him and tell him that if he continues to be part of such inhuman destructiveness he sins against creation and the Creator. Go to him and plead with him to repent and ask for mercy while there is still time to do so."

Robert McAfee Brown

This is a time when you and I need to get angry. The economy is booming. Unemployment has declined but hunger has not dropped at all since 1995. In the richest nation in the world, in the best economy of the century, 31 million people still can't count on enough food over the month to feed themselves and their children. Scandal of scandals, hunger has not declined and congress is playing political games with tax cuts that could lead to even more hunger. It's time to get angry and insist on justice for all of God's children.

David Beckmann, President,
Bread for the World

> Amos 5:21-24
>
> *I hate, I despise your feasts, and I take no delight in your solemn assemblies. Even though you offer me your burnt offerings and cereal offerings, I will not accept them, and the peace offerings of your fatted beasts I will not look upon. Take away from me the noise of your songs; to the melody of your harps I will not listen. But let justice roll down like waters, and righteousness like an everflowing stream.*

REFLECTION • ACTION

1. Can you think of any one social issue over which you have become outraged enough to speak out or take some action? Did the issue affect you directly? Or the poor and oppressed around you?

2. What are the social sins of today where our moral outrage must be directed? Compare your list with that of a friend. Who benefits if things remain as they are?

3. How can we distinguish between anger and hatred? Is there any social issue or injustice that would justify civil or ecclesial disobedience? See Exodus 1:15-17.

4. Read: *Saying Yes and Saying No,* on Rendering to God and Caesar, by Robert McAfee Brown, Westminster, 1986; and/or *The Coming of the Cosmic Christ* by Matthew Fox, Harper and Row, 1988.

FROM INDIVIDUALISM TO CONNECTEDNESS

> Even though Western society has created separation and alienation by stressing rugged individualism and material wealth, we are, essentially tribal people meant to live together, share the load and care for one another as we pass through the many phases of life.
>
> C.S. Kasl

In *Habits of the Heart* Robert Bellah has described individualism as a cancer that is destroying community values and commitment in our society. The evidence is overwhelming. In *Sharing the Journey*, Robert Wuthnow tells about the growing interest in small groups as evidence that a quiet revolution is taking place. People are sensing the need to connect with others for support and encouragement. Is there a rebellion starting to emerge against the culturally induced desire for self-centered living and independence? Why has the church been so slow in giving leadership to the importance of connectedness and community? When will the church wake up and put as much value on building community as it does on building budgets? *Earth Community – Earth Ethics* by Larry Rasmussen reminds us that we are on a collision course because we have not comprehended our human and spiritual relationship with the earth. The current environmental crisis calls for a radical shift from individualism to earth community and connectedness.

In previous chapters we have touched on the needed shift in attitudes as we find our way in the maze of issues that relate to the unnecessary suffering in the world. Perhaps awakening to our connectedness should be at the top. It has been mentioned earlier but deserves a more intentional focus. Recognizing the problems that individualism has created is the beginning. The healing continues as we begin to make the connections and begin to work towards a recognition of our earth community. What we need to work on is relationships. As Rasmussen says, "Nothing is itself without everything else."

Hal Dragseth, a friend of past years, told about a meaningful relationship he had built as a mentor-friend to a mentally disadvantaged teenager. At an Olympics event he watched from the sidelines as his friend raced around the track to see who would finish first. When his friend spotted him on the sidelines he broke from the race to come over and thank Hal for coming to the event. "No, no! Get back in the race!" he shouted. But to no avail. Competition was not as important as his relationship to his mentor, his friend. Friendship was more important than the individual honor of winning. He hadn't learned to sacrifice in order to be number one. Many in our society would call it stupid, a bad choice, living in another world. When Hal told about his experience I got teary eyed. It was a lesson in community building I will not soon forget.

There are many ways to talk about the need for connectedness in our journey of learning how to love God and neighbor. I would like to give attention to three. One would certainly be the importance of solidarity with those who are in pain and struggling to survive. It is one thing to feel sorry for them, but this may not be the same as entering into their pain and understanding a little bit of what they are going through. Some of us may even prefer feeling guilty to participating in their suffering. We might give a generous offering and forego an opportunity for a face to face encounter. To experience connectedness (solidarity) can be uncomfortable. It takes time and sometimes sacrifice. But isn't this what Jesus was about? Brueggemann talks about the love of neighbor as "othering" that belongs to the gospel. He says, "We find great resources of grace and courage for living with the neighbor, even the neighbor who is blatantly other."

Another aspect to connectedness is the way in which we are connected to the earth. Some of us have been taught a kind of gnosticism that sees matter as evil and spirit as good. Therefore, we don't sense the need to relate to earth community. Our theology as well as our cultural assumptions have focused on an anthropocentric perspective of life. We need a re-orientation. Salvation and redemption are not just related to individuals but to creation itself. The apostle Paul reminds us, "Creation waits with eager longing for the revealing of the children of light" (Romans 8:19).

At one point in history both the church and science were convinced that the sun revolved around the earth, a very anthropocentric assumption.

Copernicus and Galileo called for a shift in consciousness. The church was tied into its closed world view and its attached moral code. The Pope forced Galileo to recant and put him under house arrest. It was a sin, a form of blasphemy to suggest that earth and its occupants were not the center of everything. As in Galileo's day, so in our day we need a different cosmology, a shift in our thinking and connectedness to creation.

A third area of connectedness vital to our struggle is to understand how all the issues of social justice are related to one another. We cannot afford to maintain a lone-ranger approach. Everything is connected. We need each other. For example, we must wake up to the reality of interconnectedness of sustainable agriculture, to the cost of food, to free trade issues, and to immigration quotas. We need to be alert to how our financial investments (stocks and bonds) relate to the plight of banana pickers in Honduras and the environmental problems in countries with fewer regulations, and to child labor abuse worldwide. We need to see that how we vote, or fail to vote, is related to global economic issues, to health care for the elderly, to refugees in Africa, to third world debt relief and to campaign finance reform. We need to see how prison reform relates to racism, to poverty, to single parent issues.

It would be eye opening to pursue the connectedness of money and economics to almost every issue we hear about as it relates to living in this world. We live in a world dominated by economic thought. Jesus was not afraid to talk about it. It was more often mentioned in his message than heaven or forgiveness. If we fail to make these connections we are either in denial or will work at solutions that are short lived and beneficial only to those who are privileged. One example is the way economic development had led to even more ecological destruction. It is important to make the faith connection to this issue. Larry Rasmussen tells about a poem of Bonhoeffer written during his last months in prison which distinguishes Christians from non-Christians. Bonhoeffer wrote:"It is not a distinction from God's side. God goes to all in their need, forgives all, and for all alike, hangs dead. The distinction is from our side. Christians are those who stand by God in God's hour of grieving. What makes a Christian at all is participation in God's suffering in the secular life, joining the divine agony over the needy state of the battered creation. The Latins call it solidarity. Bonhoeffer calls it participation."

OTHER VOICES

Contribution of Hispanic Theology

Western theology – especially that which takes place in academic circles – has long suffered from an exaggerated individualism. …The methodology of a Hispanic theology will contrast with this. Ours is not a tradition that values individualism, as does that of the North Atlantic. Ours is a language that does not even have a word for that "privacy" which the dominant North American culture so values. Our theology will result from a constant dialogue among the entire community. It will not be a theology of theologians but a theology of the believers and practicing community.

Justo L. Gonzales

When you've talked with the people who are living in fear and poverty and you've held their children in your lap and you've ached as you have contemplated their future, you can't walk away and say, "It's none of our business," and still be faithful to our Lord.

David W. Preus, After a Bishop's trip to Latin America

Jeremiah 4:19-20

My anguish, my anguish! I writhe in pain! Oh, the walls of my heart! My heart is beating wildly; I cannot keep silent; for I hear the sound of the trumpet, the alarm of war. Disaster follows hard on disaster, the whole land is laid waste. Suddenly my tents are destroyed, my curtains in a moment.

Galatians 6:2

Bear one another's burdens, and so fulfill the law of Christ.

REFLECTION • ACTION

1. How is solidarity different from sympathy or pity? Think of a time when you appreciated the ministry of someone who seemed to understand your pain, who entered into your darkness.

2. Look around you right now. From your present location observe all the things in your sight or sound. Now think of those creators and providers who are responsible for what you see and hear. How are they connected? How are you connected to them? Celebrate your connectedness.

3. Take your child, your spouse, or your friend and go sit with someone who is hurting or take time to sit with nature in silence. Do not intrude or condescend. Enter into their pain (it's pain) as best you can. See *Face to Face Encounters* page 53.

4. Read *The Liberating Pulpit* by Justo Gonzalez and Catherine Gonzalez, Abington, 1994; and/or *Becoming Native to This Place* by Wes Jackson, University Press, Kentucky, 1994; and/or *Jesus, Justice and the Reign of God* by William Herzog II, Westminster John Knox Press, 2000.

COURAGE AND ACTION

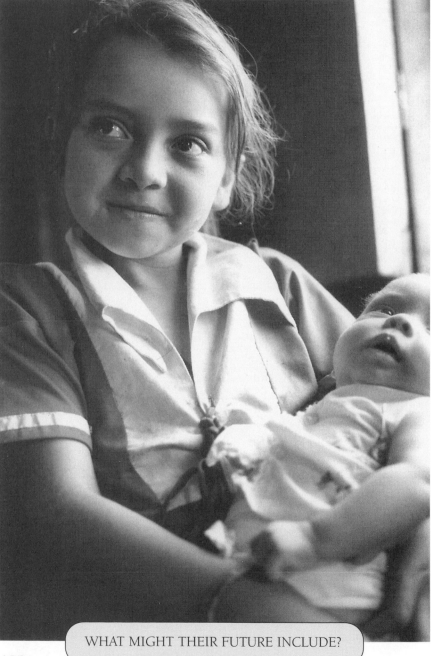

WHAT MIGHT THEIR FUTURE INCLUDE?

FROM WORDS TO THE WORD

> We are discovering that the Bible says a great deal about the poor. It all seems askew, for while the poor do get a lot of attention in the Bible, the non poor get a lot of attention in the church and usually end up running things. One reason for this is that the nonpoor have become the official interpreters of the Scriptures and have managed to take most of the sting out of the passages dealing with the poor.
>
> Robert McAfee Brown

Many of us are so bombarded with words that we despair of reading anything more about the problems of the world. Our mailboxes are full of letters asking us to join this and that cause. Pleas are made for money to help alleviate human suffering. Magazines and newspapers are full of excellent articles that both enlighten and frighten. There is no lack of words to read or voices that cry for help.

There are times when we need to set aside spoken and written words in order to encounter the Word. Not that such words aren't important. But sometimes we reach a saturation point. More information is not what is lacking, but a time to reflect or time to be alone with God, a time of silence, a time to put our inner spirit in order. From our encounters with the Word we are strengthened and better equipped to handle the call for involvement and risk-taking.

There also are times when we need to return to the Word in order to listen to those parts of Scripture that we have neglected or ignored. Our listening is enriched by recalling not only how the Word comes to us but how the Word comes to others. For example, when we listen to the Word as encountered by the poor, we hear new things because of their unique experiences. Such a word is fresh, energizing and vital to our understanding.

In order for us to move beyond guilt and powerlessness we need to search the Scriptures constantly. There we will find a God who listens to the cries of the poor, a promise of forgiveness that frees us from the burden of guilt, a Jesus who came to preach good news to the poor and set the oppressed free. In the Word we find a word of hope that sustains us when death and destruction surround us, and a young church that gave high priority to sharing with those in need. The Scriptures give us clear warnings about idolatry that causes human suffering and oppression. We are invited to participate in the kingdom where swords are beaten into plowshares and weeping is turned into songs of joy. The message within the Word dismantles the dominant consciousness of the privileged and energizes us with hope and courage to take one more step forward.

Shortly after I returned from a trip to Central America I planned my preaching for Advent and Christmas. Christians in Latin America had taught me how meaningful the magnificat passage in Luke had been to them as they struggled to survive. I decided to use the Luke 1:46-55 passage as my text for Christmas Eve. It was a first for me.

In my sermon I talked about Mary's insight and confidence that the coming messianic age would include a reversal of things. The mighty would be brought down, the lowly exalted, the rich sent away empty and the hungry would be fed good things. When I applied this message to our current situation in an affluent society I asked, "Where is the good news for us as we listen to Mary's understanding of good news?" I then laid out some ways the coming of Jesus is good news to today's world.

During my sermon, a middle aged woman walked out. I didn't think much about it. Maybe she remembered the oven was left on or she needed a potty break. After the sermon the head usher came to me with these words: "Pastor George, for eight years I've tried to get my aunt to come back to church. Tonight she came. She walked out during your sermon and said to me on the way out that she didn't come to church on Christmas Eve to hear that. She said, "That's not the Gospel." I was crushed, hurt, embarrassed and bewildered. No doubt I could have said it better but I was reminded that sometimes the Word comes to us through the words of biblical characters and it may sound strange to us because we have been protected by a cultural screening of the biblical message.

OTHER VOICES

The Power Monopoly

Peace is the redistribution of power. Any talk about peace that does not face questions of power is unbiblical. I particularly want to call your attention to the work of Norman Gottwald who, for this sort of business, is the most important Old Testament scholar we have. Gottwald has helped us see that when we open the *Bible*, we do not find a bunch of innocent nomads dressed in burlap and bathrobes, but what we find is an empire.

In Genesis 12 it says that there wasn't any bread and they went to Egypt to get bread. Now social suspicion leads one to ask: "How come Egypt had so much bread?" *What the Bible knows is that we are born into a world with social monopolies.* And what Israel wants its boys and girls to learn from little on, is that there is something wrong with social monopolies.

Genesis 47 deals with the questions: "How did we get into this mess?" "How did we get into this monopoly where some people have so much and some people don't have anything?" And there it is said: We got into it because our brother, or our alienated brother, Joseph, was a smart guy and he bought up all the land for Pharaoh.

The first year, when the poor people came for bread, he said: "I'll give you some bread and I'll take your money." The second year they needed some bread and he said: "I've got your money: I'll take your cattle." (Call that the "means of production.") The third year, when they needed some bread, he said: "I don't think you have any collateral left." So he said, "Why don't we take your land? We'll take your land and your bodies."

And they said, "Take our land and our bodies. We just don't want to starve to death. We will gladly be your slaves!"

And that is how the monopoly got established.

One very telling little footnote in Genesis 47 says that *Pharaoh took all the land except the land of the priests. (Someone has to bless the empire!)*

Exodus starts out saying that we cried out and the Lord saw and the Lord knew and the Lord remembered and the Lord came down and saved – Exodus 2, Exodus 3.

This model of peace believes that the cries of those who are excluded from the monopoly mobilize the power of justice in heaven to rearrange things.

The exodus story is the liturgical reenactment that goes on and on in families and in schools and in business and in the world – the liturgical reenactment of the redistribution of goods and the power and the access.

You know where it ends. It ends in Exodus 15:20-21, where Miriam and her sisters take timbrels and dance. The liturgy invites the community of faith from Exodus 1 to Exodus 15 to start with the cry of oppression and end with the dance of liberation. And the narrative is the enactment of the redistribution of the goods which feels (to the Israelites) like liberation and gift and miracle – but which feels to Egypt and Pharaoh like terrorism and social revolution. It all depends on where you sit when you read.

Walter Brueggemann

BIBLICAL PASSAGES RELATED TO HUNGER AND JUSTICE

Genesis 1:29-30	God gives the world's food to Adam and Eve
Exodus 3:7-12	Moses asked to go to Pharaoh
Exodus 16: 1-12	The manna life-style
Leviticus 19:9-11	Leave a portion of your harvest for the poor
Numbers 11:4-23	People greedy for meat
Deut. 14:28-15:11	A redistribution of wealth and law of tithe
1 Kings 21: 1-20	Lust for land leads to deceit and oppression
Psalm 72: 1-14	How to pray for government
Psalm 82	Justice to the weak and destitute
Psalm 146:5-9	The Lord is just and feeds the hungry
Proverbs 14:20-21	Happy are they who are kind to the poor
Proverbs 19:17	Who is kind to the poor lends to the Lord
Proverbs 21:13	Listen to the cry of the poor
Isaiah 1: 17-18	Seek justice; correct oppression
Isaiah 3: 13-15	Why do you grind the face of the poor?
Isaiah 5: 1-7	I looked for justice but beheld bloodshed
Isaiah 58:6-12	Pour yourself out for the hungry
Jeremiah 22: 13-16	To know the Lord is to do justice
Ezekiel 16:49	Sodom destroyed because of neglect of the poor
Amos 4: 1-3	Elite and wealthy women implicated in injustice
Amos 5: 10-24	Let justice roll down like waters
Amos 8:4-7	The greedy buy the poor for silver
Micah 6:8	Do justice, love mercy, walk humbly

Matthew 5:23-24	First be reconciled, then offer your gifts
Matthew 6:25-34	Seek kingdom of God and justice first
Matthew 23:23	You have neglected justice, mercy and faith
Matthew 25:31-46	I was hungry and you gave me food
Mark 8: 1-9	Feeding the multitude, also John 6: 1-14
Luke 1:46-55	Mary's Magnificat, the great reversal
Luke 10:25-37	Good Samaritan
Luke 14: 12-14	Invite the poor to your dinner
Luke 16: 19-31	Rich man and Lazarus
Luke 19: 1-10	Zacchaeus's radical generosity
John 6:25-35, 47-51	I am the bread of life
John 13:1-20	Jesus washing disciples' feet
Acts 2:42-47, 4:32-35	Sharing in the early church
Acts 6: 1-7	First dispute in church over distribution of food
I Cor. 11: 17-34	Selfishness in the Christian assembly
I Cor. 16: 1-2	Put aside for the needy
2 Cor. 8: 12-15	A question of equality and abundance
2 Cor. 9:6-15	God loves a cheerful giver
Galatians 2:10	Remember the poor
James 2: 1-7	Rich, poor and God's bias
James 2: 14 17, 26	Faith without works is dead
1 John 3:17-18	Loving in deed, not just in word
1 John 4:19-21	Cannot love God without loving neighbor

JEREMIAH 22:29

O Land, land, land! Hear the word of the Lord!

LUKE 4:18-19

The Spirit of the Lord is upon me, because he has anointed me to preach good news to the poor. He has sent me to proclaim release to the captives and recovering of sight to the blind, to set at liberty those who are oppressed, to proclaim the acceptable year of the Lord.

REFLECTION • ACTION

1. What texts from the Scriptures have been most helpful to you in the empowerment for service on behalf of human suffering? Tell when and how and by whom you were introduced to these texts.

2. Scripture can be used as escape from responsibility as well as for empowerment and comfort. Can you give any examples? What can be done to avoid using the *Bible* for escape? Discuss Brown's quote.

3. Read 2 Samuel 11:2-17 and 12:1-7. Then use your imagination and tell the story from Uriah's perspective, from Nathan's perspective, from Bethsheba's perspective, then from David's perspective. What were the issues and risks for each of them? Where are you in the story? Where is the Third World in this story?

4. Read *Unexpected News:* Reading The Bible Through Third World Eyes by Robert McAfee Brown, the Westminster Press, 1984;; and/or *Jesus Before Christianity* by Albert Nolan, Orbis, 1976; and/or *Critical Decisions in Following Jesus* by George S. Johnson, CSS Publishers, 1992; and/or *The Bible Makes Sense*, Revised Edition by Walter Brueggemann, Saint Mary's Press, 1997.

FROM CONFORMITY TO COURAGE

> *O God, make me discontent with things the way they are in the world, and in my own life. Teach me how to blush again, for the tawdry deals, the arrogant-but-courteous prejudice, the snickers, the leers, the good food and drink which make me too weary to repent, the flattery given and received, my willing use of rights and privileges other people are unfairly denied. Make me notice the stains when people get spilled on. Make me care about the slum child downtown, the misfit at work, the people crammed into the mental hospital, the men, women and youth behind bars. Jar my complacence; expose my excuses; get me involved in the life of my city, and give me integrity once more.*
>
> Robert Raines

When the apostle Paul said, "Don't be conformed to this world" (Rom. 12:1), I wonder if he knew how difficult that would be in our day. Did he have the pressures to conform (fear of unemployment, payments due, advertising, peer pressure) that we do? J. B. Philips's translation of that passage makes it even more vivid, "Don't let this world squeeze you into its mold...but be transformed." The pressures to conform are legion and powerful.

Not all conformity is bad. We are safer if we all drive on the right side of the road. It is good that most of us set aside Sunday as a day of rest and worship. But where do we draw the line? When do we decide not to conform to the norm? When do we break ranks with the majority? March to a different drum beat?

The herd instinct is strong. We tend to follow the crowd because to resist or be different is costly and risky. We don't want to stand out or call attention to ourselves. Marches or demonstrations make us too visible. We may not need new clothes but the styles have changed. Who wants to be stared at because our clothes or cars are out of style? A conversation may be flowing with ease and laughter, so why speak out for the victim or share another side of the issue and risk not being invited back? We like the security and acceptance of going with the flow.

At the same time, the poor continue to suffer and their plight worsens while many of us remain content with the status quo. "The poor you always have with you" is recalled. Without realizing it, we allow popular but faulty interpretations of Scripture to sustain our apathy and indifference.

Those who are doing something constructive are risk-takers. Rosa Parks, the black woman who refused to take a back seat on the bus in Montgomery, Alabama, was willing to risk being arrested and fined. She moved to risk-taking because conformity enabled an evil system to continue. Today she is honored as the person who ignited the great movement for civil rights that began in the 1950s.

The story of Esther in the Hebrew scriptures is a powerful example of courage, yet it has all the elements of human nature and mixed motives. Esther, after some encouragement from her uncle Mordecai, decided to go before the King to be an advocate for those condemned to die. She knew it was risky. She said, "I will go before the King though it is against the law, and, if I perish, I perish." What courage! Can she be a role model for us today?

Heroes and heroines of faith in the Scriptures all had one thing in common. They displayed courage at critical moments in their lives. They went against the stream, trusting that God would be with them. (Read Hebrews 11.) In responding to the cries of the hungry and oppressed, we often are called to act before all the evidence is in. We risk being wrong at times. That's part of the faithfulness involved in having compassion for people. No one said taking up the cross and being followers of Jesus would be risk-free.

OTHER VOICES

I Am Not an Exceptional Man

Arnold, who has made his no-questions-asked peace with the world for $30,000 ($50,000 to maybe $100,000 in today's money) a year, speaks to his ne'er-do-well brother, Murray, who has rebelled against the deceits of conventional society and cares about people passionately.

"I have long been aware, Murray...I have long been aware that you don't respect me much. I suppose there are a lot of brothers who don't get along.

"Unfortunately for you, Murray, you want to be a hero. Maybe if a fella falls into a lake, you can jump in and save him; there's still that kind of stuff. But who gets opportunities like that in midtown Manhattan, with all that traffic? I am willing to deal with the available world and I do not choose to shake it up but to live with it. There's the people who spill things, and the people who get spilled on; I do not choose to notice the stains, Murray. I have a wife and two children, and business, like they say, is business. I am not an exceptional man, so it is possible for me to stay with things the way they are. I'm lucky, I'm gifted; I have a talent for surrender. I'm at peace. But you are cursed, and I like you, so it makes me sad, you don't have the gift; and I see the torture of it. All I can do is worry for you. But I will not worry for myself; you cannot convince me that I am one of the bad guys. I get up, I go, I lie a little, I peddle a little, I watch the rules, I talk the talk. We fellas have those offices high up there so we can catch the wind and go with it, however it blows. But, and I will not apologize for it, I take pride; I am the best possible Arnold Burns."

Robert Raines, *Creative Brooding*

When is Revolt Justified?

Revolt is Christian. But we must turn to it only in cases of necessity. When people are mutiny-minded, they sometimes insist that a case of necessity exists every time something opposes their own wishes. That is why it is good that revolt or mutiny always involves great outward risk – the judgment of God.

Christians always have maintained that a willingness to suffer is a practical test in these matters of whether we are rightly related to God. Christians also have considered absolutely sinful any mutiny based solely on personal desire.

Where God's orders are trodden underfoot and the right of others to live is threatened, the Christian must be willing to go the way of sacrifice, even if it involves revolt against authority.

It is inappropriate for Christians to say that if the freedom of the church or of God's Word is not yet directly threatened, we ought not take suffering and strife upon ourselves just for the sake of "secular matters." There are no such things as "secular matters" for a Christian conscience.

Elvind Berggrav

ROMANS 12:2

Do not be conformed to this world but be transformed by the renewal of your mind, that you may prove what is the will of God, what is good and acceptable and perfect.

DANIEL 3:16-18

Shadrach, Meshach and Abednego answered the king, "O Nebuchadnezzar, we have no need to answer you in this matter. If it be so, our God whom we serve is able to deliver us from the burning fiery furnace; and he will deliver us out of your hand, O king. But if not, be it known to you, O king, that we will not serve your gods or worship the golden image which you have set up."

REFLECTION • ACTION

1. Who has modeled courage for you in their response to human suffering? What church or government leaders today demonstrate a willingness to risk for those who are considered the nobodies in society?

2. Share with others about a time when you felt you perhaps should have spoken up for someone, but didn't. What caused your silence?

3. Think through what the pressures and fears are that keep you in "conformity to the world." What are some first steps you could take to overcome those pressures, those fears? What is the source of courage? Tell about a movie or play you saw that inspired courage for you.

4. Write a letter of appreciation to someone who has demonstrated courage in helping people. Keep in correspondence with someone who is on the front lines of opposition to injustice, pain and oppression.

5. Read: *Just a Sister Away* by Renita Weems, Lura Media, 1988; and/or *Not Just Yes and Amen* by Dorothee Seolle and Fulbert Steffensky, Fortress Press, 1983; and/or *Personal History*, by Katharine Graham, Vintage Books, 1998. Suggest other related books on courage.

FROM TOO MUCH TO ENOUGH

> *If the world were merely seductive, that would be easy. If it were merely challenging, that would be no problem. But I arise in the morning, torn between a desire to save the world and a desire to savor the world. That makes it hard to plan the day!*
>
> E.B. White

One of the most difficult areas for us to deal with, in our response to hunger and poverty in the world, is our lifestyle of relative greed and over-consumption. It is far easier to give money, write letters advocating change and attend *Bible* studies on feeding the poor than to change ourselves and the way we live. Our lifestyle is connected to how we move beyond guilt, powerlessness and fear.

Most of us reading this book eat too much, buy more than we need, waste enormous amounts, consume more than our share of natural resources, and spend too much on our own security and pleasure. We constantly face the temptation to put our security in material possessions. We are told over and over again that happiness and status come from having rather than being. It is a seductive world we live in.

Peter's first epistle says of the Christian, "You have been born anew." Could it be that part of our conversion experience is to a new understanding of economics? Can we continue to support an economic system that is based on constantly expanding production of goods and services? To make it work, people must become dissatisfied or greedy so that they will buy and consume more and more. This has all kinds of implications for the environment, for our freedom from covetousness and for compassion for people on the bottom.

John Taylor, in his book *Enough is Enough*, introduces us to the theology of enough. He suggests that the dreams by which we live determine what economic systems we adopt. The law of the Sabbath, the law of the tithe, the year of jubilee, the law of the first fruits were laws of the Israelites, based on their dream of shalom for all people.

If we are to move beyond too much to enough, we will find that the issue of changing our lifestyle is important in our response to human suffering. Living more simply can be freedom for us, a freedom from insatiable appetites, as well as from the competition and success orientation that alienate us from one another. As Mary Schramm says, "Take one step at a time, but live with a renewed sense of intentionality toward patterns of living consistent with the providence of God and the vision of shalom for all God's people."

OTHER VOICES

One Person's Struggle with Lifestyle

For me it started in Detroit, at a national camp directors' meeting, where John Schramm spoke. In a very gentle, "grace-filled" way he challenged me to look at my life. On the plane ride home I thought how freeing it would be to get my life more in sync with where the gospel invites me to be.

I came home thinking (and still believe) that there is no one place that a person must start in attempting to move to a more Christ-centered lifestyle. For me, the beginning place was salary. Being a parish pastor, I have the opportunity to discuss this with my "employers" each year. I first sit down with my wife and we decide what we need in order to have "enough." The amount is not as important as the exercise in Christian stewardship we go through to arrive at our decision. It is good for our family, but also for the council and larger congregation.

The two primary challenges I face in attempting to live more simply are both close to home: my children and close relatives. The children cannot be isolated from a world that spends billions of dollars each year to convince them to consume. At ages 12 and 16, they provide some lively conversation for me as I attempt to challenge this "American way of life." Their values and mine continually are being shaped. I don't want them to take mine on as law, but I do want them to be aware of something besides the grossly consumer oriented society in which they and I live.

Larry Peterson

Pastoral Letter on U.S. Economy

America's Roman Catholic bishops issued a ringing indictment of U. S. economic realities in approving their pastoral on the economy.

"Our faith calls us to measure this economy not only by what it produces, but also by how it touches human life and whether it protects or undermines the dignity of the human person," the letter said.

"This letter is a personal invitation to American Catholics to use the resources of our faith, the strength of our economy and the opportunities of our democracy to shape a society which better protects the dignity and basic rights of our sisters and brothers in this land and around the world," the letter said.

The bishops outlined six major points:

1. Every economic decision and institution must be judged in light of whether it protects or undermines the dignity of human persons.

2. Human dignity can be realized and protected only in community.

3. All people have a right to participate in the economic life of society.

4. All members of society have a special obligation to the poor and vulnerable.

5. Human rights are the minimum conditions for life in community.

6. Society, as a whole, acting through public and private institutions, has the moral responsibility to enhance human dignity and protect human rights.

While recognizing that their statements would anger some, the bishops said, "In analyzing the economy, we reject ideological extremes, and start from the fact that ours is a 'mixed' economy, the product of a long history of reform and adjustment."

The letter also says, "The challenge of this pastoral letter is not merely to think differently, but also to act differently. A renewal of economic life depends on the conscious choices and commitments of individual believers who practice their faith in the world."

Martha Sawyer Allen,
from the Minneapolis *Star and Tribune*

JEREMIAH 22:13-16

Woe to him who builds his house by unrighteousness, and his upper rooms by injustice; who makes his neighbor serve him for nothing, and does not give him his wages; who says, 'I will build myself a great house with spacious upper rooms, paneling it with cedar, and painting it with vermilion.' Do you think you are a king because you compete in cedar? Did not your father eat and drink and do justice and righteousness? Then it was well with him. He judged the cause of the poor and needy; then it was well. Is not this to know me? says the Lord.

REFLECTION • ACTION

1. John Taylor suggests that we join the cheerful revolution of resisting rampant consumerism. How can we do this cheerfully? What benefits would consuming less have for you? For your neighbor in need? For the environment?

2. What economic decisions did you make this past month? Measure them against the six major points of the Bishops' Pastoral Letter on the U.S. Economy.

3. What dream forms our economics? Consider setting aside 1% of your income (over and above your weekly offering to your church) for causes that help the poor. Start giving away things you don't need or use. Check with Alternatives (see #4) on how your church can find alternative ways to observe Christmas.

4. Read *Simplicity-The Art of Living* by Richard Rohr, Crossroad Publishing, 2000; and/or *To Celebrate* and *Simple Living 101*, a tool for sharing the joy of a simpler lifestyle from Alternatives, Box 2857, Sioux City, IA 51106, 1-800-821-6153. Alternatives also has other resources for those struggling with lifestyle issues;; and/or *God, Good and the Common Good*, Eleven Perspectives on Economic Justice, edited by Charles P. Lutz, Augsburg, 1987; and/or *Following Christ in a Consumer Society* by John Francis Kavanaugh, Orbis, 1981.

FROM DOMINION TO STEWARDSHIP

> *The deterioration of the environment is an outward mirror of an inner condition – like inside, like outside. As we go through the checklist of environmental problems – from Chernobyl to Three Mile Island, from Love Canal to an agricultural landscape strewn with agrichemicals and uncontrolled soil erosion – one thing becomes increasingly clear: that we of the Judeo-Christian tradition have failed miserably to meet the assignment of the first work task given our forebears, "to care for the garden."*
>
> Wes Jackson

The metaphor of the "steward" carries important meaning for us in our search for a lifestyle appropriate to our calling as Christians. Douglas John Hall in his book *The Steward*, a Biblical Symbol Come of Age, has suggested that stewardship is a way of conceiving the mission of the Christian movement in the post-Christian era. He contends that understanding stewardship is the key to our understanding the mission of seeking justice, peace and integrity of creation.

The movie *Oh God!* had profound insights related to stewardship. The manager of the market (played by John Denver) received a message from God (played by George Burns) to give to the world. But no one would listen, including religious people. The message God wanted to deliver was simple. "I'm here. I still like you a lot. It can work (meaning the harmony and laws of nature in the universe which God set in order). And don't hurt one another." A good steward is one who believes that and lives accordingly. The movie presents a simple message with gospel and responsibility carefully balanced.

The biblical understanding of stewardship implies accountability and participation. To move beyond guilt and powerlessness, we need to move from mastery, control and ownership attitudes to an attitude of stewardship toward all of life. This means becoming caretakers of creation with a sense of identification and partnership, rather than domination and exploitation. To be a steward of creation is to embrace the world, to love the world as Christ did, and to be willing to sacrifice for the world rather than escape from the world.

The Shakertown Pledge was the outcome of a gathering of committed people seeking ways to respond to the cry for eco-justice. Notice its concern for accountability and participation.

THE SHAKERTOWN PLEDGE

Recognizing that the earth and the fullness thereof is a gift from our gracious God, and that we are called to cherish, nurture and provide loving stewardship for the earth's resources,

And recognizing that life itself is a gift, and a call to responsibility, joy and celebration, I make the following declarations:

1. I declare myself to be a world citizen.

2. I commit myself to lead an ecologically sound life.

3. I commit myself to lead a life of creative simplicity and to share my personal wealth with the world's poor.

4. I commit myself to join with others in reshaping institutions in order to bring about a more just global society in which each person has full access to the needed resources for their physical, emotional, intellectual and spiritual growth.

5. I commit myself to occupational accountability, and in so doing I will seek to avoid the creation of products which cause harm to others.

6. I affirm the gift of my body, and commit myself to its proper nourishment and physical well-being.

7. I commit myself to examine continually my relations with others and to attempt to relate honestly, morally and lovingly to those around me.

8. I commit myself to personal renewal through prayer, meditation, and study.

9. I commit myself to responsible participation in a community of faith.

OTHER VOICES

Living in Harmony

Mother Earth is in jeopardy, caused by the anthropocentrism of religion, education and science during the past three centuries. A new beginning is required, centered on the sacredness of the planet – its rainforests, oceans, soil, air and all the creatures of the Earth.

I believe that religion, science and art must overcome their antagonisms and work together to awaken the human imagination and to heal the planet. The survival of the Earth depends upon "reinventing our species" (Thomas Berry) so that we live more harmoniously with nature. The new cosmology that science, art and mysticism unite to teach is the ancient spiritual and ecological lesson: All things are connected.

Matthew Fox

A New Agriculture

We are asking an awesome question in this book: Will there be food for tomorrow? The outcome of the world food crisis, as well as the future course of American agriculture, depends on whether the constant resource abuse of the world can be stopped. This hoped-for reversal depends most fundamentally on whether we humans are able to shift from relating to the sustaining resources of the created world as objects of exploitation to seeing resources as subjects of God's order.

But is reversal possible? Where can we get help? The ancient wisdom of the biblical tradition provides a firm basis for building a needed ethic for our time. In this wisdom are found fundamental insights for establishing the criteria (value, attitude, measurement, policy) for a new agriculture, an agriculture that can move us beyond the dominant destructive trends of contemporary practice into a preferred future.

C. Dean Freudenberger,
Food for Tomorrow?

LUKE 12:42

And the Lord said, "Who then is the faithful and wise steward, whom his master will set over his household, to give them their portion of food at the proper time? Blessed is that servant whom his master when he comes will find so doing.

PSALM 24:1

The earth is the Lord's and the fullness thereof, the world and they that dwell therein.

REFLECTION • ACTION

1. What area of abuse to the created order (biotic community) have you become most concerned about? Why has it concerned you? What are you doing about it?

2. Which part of the Shakertown Pledge have you already taken? What would be the next step you need to take?

3. Do something concrete that will put you more in touch with nature and connect you with the importance of care of the earth. What can we learn from the American Indians about our relationship to the earth?

4. Read *Dream of the Earth* by Thomas Berry, Sierra Club Books, 1988, and/or *Patching God's Garment*-Environment and Mission in the 21st Century by W. Dayton Roberts, MARC World Vision, 1994; and/or *Global Dustbowl* by C. Dean Freudenberger, Augsburg,1991; and/or *The Steward* by Douglas John Hall, Eerdmans, 1990; and/or *Cry of the Earth, Cry of the Poor* by Leonardo Boff, Orbis, 1997.

FROM PEACE TO PEACEMAKER

> My conscience I have from God and cannot give to Caesar.
>
> John Milton
>
> The ultimate weakness of violence is that it is a descending spiral, begetting the very thing it seeks to destroy. Instead of diminishing evil, it multiplies it...Returning violence for violence multiplies violence, adding deeper darkness to a night already devoid of stars. Darkness cannot drive out darkness; only light can do that. Hate cannot drive out hate; only love can do that.
>
> Rev. Martin Luther King, Jr.

It's a safe bet that a large majority of people favor peace over war. Despite what we favor, war is real and preparation for war is approved as a necessary deterrent. With so much of our national income going for defense spending, we are compelled to ask: Is this peacemaking?

There is a difference between peaceloving and peacemaking. One can be for peace but never really be a maker of peace. Our involvement in a largely defense economy is a seductive force in our society. We all seem to benefit either directly or indirectly from greater defense spending. It is difficult to resist something that works in our favor.

Each of us needs to think through our commitment to peace making and non-violence in both our work and leisure. How much have we been manipulated to fear our most recent "enemy," so that the weapon systems will go forward? As talks advance to reverse the arms race, what are we willing to do to make it happen? What are we willing to risk in our efforts of peacemaking?

Martin Luther King, Jr. not only spoke out strongly for civil rights, he also became an anti-war activist. Tom Witt, Director of the Lutheran Peace Fellowship said this about Dr. King: "The witness of Dr. King may embody the model we desperately need in this country for one united peace and justice movement, where each issue becomes interconnected. By 1967, one year before his assassination, Martin Luther King was speaking out not only against racism and poverty, but had expanded his critique to include militarism as one of the great evils to be challenged in American society. He became a critic of the Vietnam war and of American foreign policy in general, identifying his government as 'the greatest purveyor of violence in the world.' At home King maintained that a nation which continues year after year to spend more money on military defenses than on programs of social uplift is approaching spiritual death."

OTHER VOICES

The Demonstrator

She's a private person.
    Not one to call attention to herself.
    Never one to publicly criticize others.
    Careful, gracious behavior
    is her style.
Before acting, she asks,
    "What would the neighbors think?"

She's a believing person.
    A church-going,
    Mission-supporting,
    Bible-study leading
    Seventy-seven-year-old person of faith.
Before acting, she asks,
    "What would God think?"

She's a trusting person.
    A government-supporting,
    Law-abiding,
    Voting,
    Patriotic citizen.
Before acting, she asks,
    "Is it democratic?"

She's a genteel person.
    A wisp of a smile
    Lays in a puff of soft white skin.

Two tender blue eyes peek out,
Open to faces around her.
Her attire belies her destination today:
A ribbon-trimmed, wide-brimmed hat
Accentuates white permed hair.
A crisp white suit with blue trim
Clothes her round frame.
White-washed high heels
Complete the look.
Is she going to a luncheon, a fashion show? No!
She's going to a parade.
She's going to *march* in a parade.

It's not much of a parade.
Twelve marchers...
If you count the baby
In the stroller.

At the head of the parade,
Behind the police escort
With his gaudy, blinking light,
Stands our unlikely demonstrator.

Shyly she greets her marching partner,
Then begins to converse:
"My son went to war.
When he came home, I said,
'John, you're so thin!'

"'Mom,'" he replied,
"I've got my arms, my legs.
I can see and hear.
Just be glad I'm home.'"
Her partner nods, with tears.

Then – with strong resolve –
Our demonstrator states:
"We who raise children
Should *refuse* to send them off to war!"

The parade begins.
Forward it moves.
A private person takes a public stance.
A believing, trusting, genteel person
Marches in her high heels
Right down Main Street
Holding a banner high.
A banner with large red letters:
MOTHERS' PEACE MARCH!

Vivian Elaine Johnson

Where to Start

Right after I left the weapons industry, I wrote an article about things that motivated me to leave. One of my friends who still worked at Lockheed took this article to work and put a routing slip on it and circulated it among the engineers I used to work with. Various ones wrote little comments on the back of the routing slip. When my friend received it back, after everybody had read and initialed it, he sent me the routing slip with the comments. Another friend there had written that "This ideology is correct indeed." In other words, he agreed with what I had written, but he thought it would have to be accepted by the whole world in order to have any meaningful effect. And then he ended with, "The question is where to start?" I think that if I were to answer that question, I would say that the place to start is with yourself, because you're responsible for what you're doing. When you begin to change your own life to live more according to those ideals that most, if not all, people hold, then it becomes very apparent what effect that one person can have.

In the Pacific Life Community with which I once worked in resisting injustices, we treated nonviolence as not only a tactic or a public witness, but also as a personal issue. We felt, and I still feel, that nonviolence starts first within – by rearranging the lifestyle to be less exploitive. Before we can overcome the military mindset and system that threatens global destruction, we must first overcome the ignorance and apathy within us that prevent us from relating to our brothers and sisters in this country and all over the world.

Robert Aldridge

A Prayer from Haiti

Dear God, in the past – and still in our time – the church has given its blessing to the sword. Forgetting that the gates of hell shall never prevail against her, the church has developed "policies of survival" and become "security addicted."

We weep, O God, for a church so afraid of dying that it has compromised itself with the powers of this world. We weep for a church that sells its soul for "protection" and "peace" and the "freedom" to preach a heavenly gospel – so long as it does nothing to disturb the repressive, law-and-order society around it.

Ransom us, we pray. Ransom us so that we may at last, with you and your Spirit, enter Zion singing.

Roger Desir

MATTHEW 5:9

Blessed are the peacemakers, for they shall be called sons of God.

MICAH 6:8

He has showed you, O man, what is good; and what does the Lord require of you but to do justice, and to love kindness, and to walk humbly with your God?

REFLECTION • ACTION

1. Can you think of times when your yes to God has meant saying no to some present accepted system or value in society? How has your no been borne out in your actions? What were the results?

2. National security is important to each nation. At what point does national security become an opponent to peacemaking, to the Christian faith? Can one relate King's quote about violence to capital punishment?

3. Decide to do one special thing each month for the next year as a peacemaking effort. Ask your church to begin a peacemaking support group, and become one of its members. Sing or pray the World Peace Prayer each day, see page 135.

4. Read *The Politics of Jesus* by John Howard Yoder, Eardmans, 1994; and/or *The Arms Race Kills Even Without War* by Dorothee Soelle, Fortress, 1983 and/or *ProLife – ProPeace* by Lowell Erdahl, Augsburg, 1986; and/or *Of War and Love* by Dorothee Soelle, Orbis, 1983; and/or *Nuclear Madness* by Helen Caldicott, Autumn Press, 1978.

FROM STATUS QUO TO ENCOUNTER

> *O God, make me love justice, and seek equal job opportunity where I work, open housing in my apartment building or suburb, open membership in my club, better schools for all children in my city.*
>
> *O God, make me hate wrong and speak out against it boldly, at parties, among my relatives, in my church board meetings, at work.*
>
> *O God, keep me from being contentious, but make me care enough to contend for justice, against wrong, with humility.*
>
> Robert Raines

Almost all of us who have had our global consciousness raised run into friends, relatives, or neighbors who don't understand or don't appreciate our new perspective on various issues. It can be frustrating to explain to people what's happening to us, what we've learned, what we now view more critically, what new questions we've learned to ask, and what we have come to appreciate. Sometimes it seems best to remain silent, change the subject, or only touch the surface in our conversations about what we know will be controversial issues.

There is a time to be silent and a time to speak, a time to build and a time to tear down, a time to laugh and a time to cry – so says the wisdom writer of old. The important thing is to know which time it is. Most difficult is to find the courage to speak at the right time, knowing that to be totally silent is a betrayal of those who suffer.

For example, conversing with close friends and relatives about life-and-death issues that touch on politics and economics can be one of the most difficult aspects of our Christian witness. Yet such encounters are vitally important to our own integrity, our faithfulness to Christ, and our solidarity with the poor.

When we witness exploitation and oppression, silent coexistence often is deadly. In these situations it is not our lives at stake, but the lives of millions in oppressive situations whose suffering continues because people like us have not been willing to speak up.

We need to address this challenge imaginatively. In spite of intense differences, we can create accepting environments where significant issues facing Christians can be discussed and explored. As Jean Martensen says, "With God's help we can begin to transform our current arenas of tight-lipped coexistence into encounters that are both dynamic and faithful."

E. Stanley Jones, the great twentieth century evangelist and missionary to India made these recommendations for those desiring to confront racism in our society:

- Cease making "sticking" labels on whole peoples.
- Deliberately cultivate friendships with people of another race.
- Deliberately set out to find what you can learn from people of another race.
- Deliberately try to bring people of other races into your church fellowship.
- Deliberately identify yourself with the dispossessed and discriminated against, and make their disabilities your own, until everything is thrown open to everyone on the basis of equal opportunity to all.

OTHER VOICES

My Brother and I Disagree

My brother and I rarely agree on anything. The issues that polarize the American public tend to divide us too. Since our daughters were quite young when we moved to Geneva, Switzerland, I had not expected them to retain clear memories of the argumentative but fun-loving, good-natured uncle who helped us resettle in the United States. After seven years abroad with the Lutheran World Federation, I imagined our homecoming would find them as unprepared for him as they were.

Uncle John, our daughters quickly learned, was an unrepentant prankster. In public and in private, he left them laughing and redfaced. After a few short days together, however, they not only learned to accept this zany uncle from Phoenix but also to retaliate with sly jokes of their own. His unpredictable humor, I soon discovered, was not the source of their bewilderment.

What they found difficult to understand was how their uncle could be so different from their mother. Even harder to fathom was why these profound differences did not appear to threaten our relationship. Years later they still recall with wonder the night we lit the candles on the picnic table and argued – with considerable passion – for six straight hours about every topic imaginable: presidential politics, the international economy, the handling of hostages, immigration policies, causes of unemployment, environmental pollution, the role of religion in American life, the women's movement and its impact on us and our families, and more.

After years of virtually no contact, the list of concerns seemed inexhaustible. Too, the time abroad had furnished me with a global perspective on every subject that surfaced. It was as difficult for me to eliminate this consciousness from our discussion as it was for my brother to see its relevance to the case he was making. Yet, as divisive as these issues were, they never obliterated the unspoken rules of the debate. It was always equally important to both of us

- to affirm the other and to give each other space,
- to be aware of our feelings,
- to name and explore the real problems,
- to laugh at ourselves,
- to obtain both new information and new insights in the course of the exchange, to empathize with each other,
- to discover areas of mutual interest, and
- to create new possibilities together.

Why? How did we come to rely on this unarticulated methodology? As children, I think, my brother and I gradually integrated this way of dealing with those who differed from us through a combination of historical demands, familial values and exposure to the gospel of Jesus Christ.

Jean Martensen

I believe there is a time for patience and a time for impatience; a time for obedience and a time for disobedience – or a deeper obedience than that exacted by human laws and institutions. There is a time for continuity and a time for discontinuity. Ours are times – because of the unprecedented crises of Mother Earth, of our youth, of the spiritual vacuity of institutional Christianity in Europe, of the boredom that most worship instills in persons – for holy impatience, disobedience and discontinuity.

Matthew Fox

A Letter to the President

Dear Mr. President:

I am a farmer, the son of a German immigrant who was so proud to become a citizen of the United States. During August 16-27 I traveled to Mexico, Honduras and Nicaragua to get firsthand information about problems concerning world hunger. I am now very concerned that my tax dollars are being spent in military aid to Latin American governments that suppress the opportunity for the poor in society to develop. The people we had contact with did not want war. They wanted to be left alone to develop their society in their own way. This is the first time I have ever spoken out in this way. I have, in the past, felt our government was usually on the right track. After seeing and hearing firsthand from so many people, I feel I must not remain quiet.

John Everts, Iowa farmer

COLOSSIANS 4:6

Let your speech always be gracious, seasoned with salt, so that you may know how you ought to answer every one.

EXODUS 3:10

Come, I will send you to Pharaoh that you may bring forth my people, the sons of Israel, out of Egypt.

REFLECTION • ACTION

1. Reflect on the rules of the debate Jean Martensen uses in her encounters with relatives. Which are the more difficult for you? Why? How can these be applied to congregations as well as individuals?

2. What does it mean to be politicized? Can one be faithful to the gospel without getting involved in political issues? Who are the pharaohs in today's society that need to be addressed with the words "Let God's people go?"

3. Write a letter to one of your elected leaders in Washington D.C. Share your concern for a particular issue before Congress that impacts the poor or the environment. Their addresses are: U. S. House of Representatives, Washington, D.C. 20515. U.S. Senate, Washington D.C. 20510.

4. Become a member of Bread for the World, a Christian citizens' movement that informs people of legislative issues impacting hungry people. Address: 50 F Street NW, Suite 500, Washington, DC 20001, 1-888-297-2767.

5. Read *Meeting Jesus Again for the First Time* by Marcus Borg, Harper, 1994 and/or *Speaking of Christianity* – Practical Compasion, Social Justice and Other Wonders by Robert McAfee Brown, Westminster John Knox, 1997; and/or *I Asked For Wonder*, A Spiritual Anthology by Abraham Joshua Heschel, edited by Samuel H. Dresner, Crossroads, 1998.

AFTERWORD AND BIBLIOGRAPHY

MORE THAN 30,000 CHILDREN IN THE WORLD
DIE EACH DAY OF HUNGER OR RELATED DISEASES.
WHO WILL SPEAK FOR THEM?

FROM GOOD FRIDAY TO EASTER

> When our preaching about the poor stops being preaching and becomes our living on behalf of the poor, then Easter is taken from the realm of myth and becomes a powerful movement on the plane of history where poverty brings an early death to so many people. And when we, as Easter people, stand up and say no to poverty, no to hunger, no to unemployment, we are robbing death of its power. When we stand up on behalf of the poor and of every person victimized by injustice, we are saying the future is not closed. No lie can live forever. When we take our hammers and saws and bend our backs to transform shacks into affordable housing for people who never dreamed of living somewhere all their own, we are testifying to the light that has come into the world to enlighten every person. "No lie can live forever."
>
> Kenneth Wheeler

Death and resurrection have always been at the heart of the Judeo-Christian faith. It predates Calvary and the empty tomb. The idea of darkness and dawn, pain and healing, loss and newness has been part of the creation's history from the beginning. Out of chaos and darkness God created something beautiful and good. We all were born into this world following labor and pain. Birthing always comes after struggle.

Throughout these chapters we have been reminded that we are people of hope who have been given energy for life. This energy is born out of the experience of struggle, frustration and grief. The oppression and death of so many people overwhelms us. In one way or another we identify with Rachel, who grieved over the loss of her children.

> **JEREMIAH 31:15**
>
> *A voice is heard in Ramah, lamentation and bitter weeping. Rachel is weeping for her children; she refuses to be comforted for her children because they are not.*

We grieve over the millions who needlessly die of hunger. The environment is crying out in pain because of exploitation. Feelings of guilt, powerlessness and fear, as well as anger, despair and anguish, could lead us to look for an easier way. There is always the strong temptation to find an escape from Good Friday in order to come to Easter.

Many churches have neglected or glorified Good Friday so that the greater emphasis could be placed on the resurrection. This is a mistake. No wonder there is a great deal of denial of reality or avoidance of grief over the injustice, oppression and pain being experienced by so much of God's creation today. Making Christianity an otherworldly religion is an example of our denial of both Good Friday and Easter. To preach the cross without reference to the cross in today's world is to miss the message of Jesus who called us to take up the cross.

We are Easter people living in a Good Friday world. But there is no Easter until there is Good Friday. Not until we are willing to embrace the pain will we experience newness and power for healing. There is no hope if we quickly rush to the empty tomb without lingering at the cross. In our urge for order, security and peace of mind, we may clamor for signs of hope that suggest the possibility of new life without grief and pain, without the cross.

Elie Wiesel has observed that the survivors of the Holocaust in Europe during World War II are precisely the ones who can yet believe in God, a God who suffers and cares. Other Jews who have not experienced such hurt doubt more easily. Perhaps it is no different for us Christians who crowd our churches on Easter without any experience of Good Friday. We are more prone to accept the status quo without criticism, protest, or grief.

The metaphor of Sarah is taken up by Isaiah when he announces to the exiles in Chapter 54 that things will be different. When it seems hopeless, a word of hope is given. When there seems to be no way out, the prophet announces that God will intervene. The barren one will have children.

> ISAIAH 54:1
>
> *Sing O barren one, who did not bear; break forth into singing and cry aloud, you who have not been in travail! For the children of the desolate one will be more than the children of her that is married, says the Lord.*

The biblical message of hope is one of surprise and newness that comes in the midst of despair and pain. It is a word that comes to those who have exhausted all other resources. This word of promise gives a fresh imagination of how things can be different. This hope enables us to believe in and work for a world of justice, equity, freedom and shalom, because our God is free to act beyond the visible constructs of our present system.

The truths of Good Friday and Easter, once experienced, give us a new capacity to resist the forms of power that absolutize earthly systems, systems that favor some at the expense of others. We act in new ways, we carry on with a different vision, an enlightened imagination, even when there is little evidence that our dream will become a reality.

So we do not lose heart. We may be "afflicted in every way, but not crushed; struck down but not destroyed, perplexed but not driven to despair, persecuted but not forsaken, always carrying in the body the death of Jesus, so that the life of Jesus may be manifested in our bodies" (2 Corinthians 4:8-10). We continue to sing the doxology as our lives bear witness to this Easter hope.

A number of Christians and others have covenanted together to sing or say the following prayer once a day as a way of remembering that we are Easter people living in a Good Friday world.

> *Lead us from death to life, from falsehood to truth, from despair to hope, from fear to trust. Lead us from hate to love, from war to peace. Let peace fill our hearts. Let peace fill our world. Let peace fill our universe.*
>
> Mother Teresa

The Fellowship of Reconciliation recommends the praying of the World Peace Prayer at the noon meal so that a continuous chain of prayer for peace is offered daily.

DREAMING UPSIDE DOWN

I dreamed the other night that all the maps in the world had been turned upside down. Library atlases, roadmaps of Cincinnati, wall-sized maps in war rooms of great nations, even antique maps inscribed "Here be Dragons" were all flipped over. What had been north was now south, east was west. Like melting vanilla ice cream, Antarctica now capped schoolroom globes.

In my dream a cloud of anxieties closed around me. The United States was now at the bottom. Would we have to stand upside down, causing the blood to rush to our heads? Would we need suction-cup shoes to stay on the planet and would autumn leaves fall up? No, I remembered, the apple bopped Newton on the head – no need to worry about these things.

Other matters troubled me more. Now that we're at the bottom, would our resources and labor be exploited by the new top? Would African, Asian and Latin American nations structure world trade to *their* advantage?

Would my neighbors and I have two-dollar-a-day seasonal jobs on peach and strawberry plantations? Would the women and children work from dawn to dusk to scratch survival from the earth of California and Virginia? Would the fruit we picked be shipped from New Orleans and New York to Thai and Ethiopian children who hurriedly eat it with their cereal so they won't miss the school bus? Would our children, then, go not to school but to fetch water from two miles away and to gather wood for cooking and heating? Would a small ruling class in this country send their daughters and sons to universities in Cairo and Buenos Aires?

Would our economy be dependent upon the goodwill and whims of, say, Brazil? Would Brazil send war planes and guns to Washington

D.C. to assure our willingness to pick apples, pecans and tobacco for export while our children went hungry? Would Brazil or Vietnam fight their wars with our sons in our country? Would we consider revolution?

If we did revolt, would the Chilean government plot to put their favorite U.S. general in power and uphold him with military aid?

Would we work in sweatshops to manufacture radios for the Chinese? Would our oil be shipped in tankers to Southeast Asia to run cars, air-conditioners and microwave ovens while most of our towns were without electricity?

Would religious leaders from "the top-of-the-world" call us stubborn pagans upon whom God's judgment had fallen, causing our misery? Would they proclaim from their opulent pulpits that if we simply turned to God, our needs would be met?

In my dream, I saw a child crying in Calcutta. Her parents wouldn't buy her any more video games until her birthday. I saw her mother drive to the supermarket and load her cart with junk food, vegetables, cheese, meat and women's magazines.

I saw a mother in Houston baking bread in an earthen oven. She had been crying because there were no more beans for her family. One of her children, a blond boy about six years old, listlessly watched her. He slowly turned his empty, haunting gaze toward me.

At that I awoke with a gasp. I saw I was in my own bed, in my own house. Everything was okay. It was a bad dream. I drifted back to sleep, thinking, "It's all right, I'm still on top."

Thank God!

Tom Peterson, Editor, Seeds

CREDITS

Every effort has been made to trace the ownership of all material and to secure the permissions necessary to reprint these selections. Unless otherwise noted, all excerpts from personal correspondence refer to correspondence from the individual noted to George S. Johnson. We are grateful to the following individuals and publishers who have granted permission to reproduce their materials in *Beyond Guilt*.

Introduction: Personal correspondence from Tom Soeldner.

Chapter 1: Quote by *Carter Heyward from Lutheran Human Relations Association of America 1988 Calendar*; used by permission of LHRAA, 2703 N. Sherman Blvd., Milwaukee, WI 53210. Personal correspondence from Tom Soeldner. Quote from "The Biblical Concept of Justice" presented by Rolf Knierem to The ALC South Pacific District Convention.

Chapter 2: Quote from *Markings* by Dag Hammarskjold, translated by Leif Sjoberg and W. H. Auden; ©1964 Alfred A. Knopf, Inc. and Faber and Faber Ltd. Sermon by Ernest T. Campbell. Quote from *The Cost of Discipleship* by Dietrich Bonhoeffer; ©1959 SCM Press, Ltd; used by permission of SCM Press, Ltd. and Macmillan Publishing Company. Personal correspondence from Deborah Peters.

Chapter 3: Quotes from the article "Theological Education: Healing the Blind Beggar" by Walter Brueggemann in *The Christian Century*, February 5-12, 1986 ©1986 The Christian Century; used by permission. Quotes from the article "Yesterday's Victims Forgotten, Struggle Is on for Today's" by Elie Wiesel.

Chapter 4: Quote by Greg Ogden from *The New Reformation*, page 11, ©1990, Zondervan. Quote by E. Stanley Jones from *The Reconstruction of the Church-On What Pattern*, page 46, ©1970, Abingdon. Used by permission.

Chapter 5: Quote from "The Pathway of Peace: Father (Abuna Elias) Chacour," *SCAN* #521, Part 1, December 22, 1985. Quote by Dorothy Day from the *ELCA Hunger Program Newsletter*, Winter 1989.

Chapter 6: Quote from *Hopeful Imagination: Prophetic Voices in Exile* by Walter Brueggemann, ©1986 Fortress Press. Article "We Sing Mary's Song" by Bonnie Jensen from *Word & World*, July 1987; used by permission of Bonnie Jensen and Luther Northwestern Theological Seminary, St. Paul, Minn.

Chapter 9: Personal correspondence from Don Christensen. Personal correspondence from Marilyn Borchardt. Article "Face to Face Encounters" from *Evangelism and the Poor* by Ana De Garcia and George S. Johnson, ©1986 The

American Lutheran Church. Quote by Chad Meyers from *I Will Call You, OK?* Used by permission.

Chapter 10: Quote by John B. Cobb, Jr. from *Grace and Responsibility* page 11, ©1995, Abingdon. Quote by Bill Williams from *Naked Before God*, ©1998, Moorehouse. Quote by Evelyn and James D. Whitehead in Expressions magazine, October/November 1987, © Whitehead Associates, 19120 Oakmont S. Dr., South Bend, IN 46637.

Chapter 11: Quote from *Ill Fares the Land* by Susan George, © 1984 Institute for Policy Studies (enlarged, revised edition to be issued by Penguin Books in 1990). Quote by Elsa Tamez from *The Bible of the Oppressed,* © 1982 Orbis Books. Quote from Frances Moore Lappe from *Food Monitor*, Winter 1988; used by permission of Food First/Institute for Food and Development Policy, 145 Ninth St., San Francisco, CA 94103.

Chapter 12: Quote by Barbara Ward and Rene DuBois from *Only One Earth*, page 12, ©1972, W.W. Norton.

Chapter 13: Quote by Douglas John Hall from *Why Christian?* ©1998, Augsburg Fortress. Quote by Jim Wallis from *Faith Works*, page 6, ©2000, Random House. Quote by John S. Spong from *Why Christianity Must Change or Die*, ©1998, Harper/Collins.

Chapter 14: Quote by Ron Sider from *Just Generosity*, pages 221-222, ©1999, Baker Books.

Chapter 15: Quote from *City of Joy* by Dominque LaPierre, © 1985 Doubleday & Company.

Chapter 16: Quote by Henri Nouwen from a special edition of *World Peacemakers* entitled "Henri Nouwen: Call to Peacemaking"; used by permission of World Peacemakers, 2025 Massachusetts Ave. N. W., Washington, D.C. 20036. Article"Justice and Economics: A Third World View" by Judith Moore from *Lutheran Women*, March 1984, © 1984 Lutheran Church Women.

Chapter 17: Quote by Susan George from *CWS Connections*, Vol. 4, No. 1, ©1987 Church World Service. Quote by George S. Johnson from the pamphlet "Africa on Fire". Quote from *Saying Yes and Saying No* by Robert McAfee Brown, © 1986 Westminster Press; used by permission of Westminster/John Knox Press. Quote by David Beckmann from letter to members of Bread for the World, used by permission.

Chapter 18: Quote by Larry L. Rasmussen from *Global Perspectives: A Newsletter of the Center for Global Education*, July/August 1987. Quote by Justo Gonzales from *Mañana*, pages 29-30, ©1990, Abingdon. Used by permission.

BIBLIOGRAPHY

Balasuriya, Tissa. *The Eucharist and Human Liberation*. Orbis, 1977

Banquet of Praise Songs and Prayers. Bread for the World, 1990

Baranowski, Arthur. *Creating Small Faith Communities*. Bethany Press, 1988

Beckmann, David and Simon, Arthur. *Grace at the Table*. Intervarsity, 1995

Berry, Thomas. *The Dream of the Earth*. Sierra Club, 1988

Boff, Leonardo. *Cry of the Earth, Cry of the Poor*. Orbis, 1997

Borg, Marcus. *Meeting Jesus Again for the First Time*. Harper Collins, 1994

Borg, Marcus. *The God We Never Knew*. Harper Collins, 1997

Bosch, David. *Transforming Mission*. Orbis, 1992

Boucher, Douglas. Editor: *The Paradox of Plenty*. Food First Books, 1999

Bradshaw, Bruce. *Bridging the Gap*. MARC World Vision, 1993

Brown, Robert McAfee. *Saying Yes and Saying No*. Rendering to God and Ceasar. Westminster, 1986

Brown, Robert McAfee. *Speaking of Christianity*. Westminster John Knox, 1997

Brown, Robert McAfee. *Unexpected News*. Reading the *Bible* through Third World Eyes. Westminster, 1984

Brueggemann, Walter. *The Bible Makes Sense*. Saint Mary's Press, 1997

Brueggemann, Walter. *Cadences of Home*. Westminster John Knox, 1997

Brueggemann, Walter. *Prophetic Imagination*. Fortress, 1978

Brueggemann, Walter. *The Covenanted Self*. Fortress, 1999

Brueggemann, Walter, Parks and Groome. *To Act Justly, Love Tenderly, Walk Humbly*. Paulist Press, 1986

Buechner, Fredrick. *The Longing For Home*. Harper, 1996

Campolo, Tony. *Revolution and Renewal*. Westminster John Knox, 2000

Cobb, John B. Jr. and Daly, Herman. *For the Common Good*. Beacon Press, 1994

Cobb, John B. Jr. *Grace and Responsibility*. Abingdon, 1995

Crosby, Michael. *Do You Love Me?* Jesus Questions the Church. Orbis, 2000

Dawn, Marva and Peterson, Eugene. *The Unnecessary Pastor*. Eerdmans, 2000

Dorr, Donal. *Option for the Poor*. Macmillan/Orbis, 1983

Duck, Ruth, editor. *Bread for the Journey*. Pilgrim Press, 1981

Economic Justice for All. Pastoral Letter on Catholic Social Teaching and U.S. Economy. National Conference of Catholic Bishops

Elkins, David. *Beyond Religion*. Quest Books, 1998

Erdahl, Lowell. *Pro Life-Pro Peace*. Augsburg, 1986

Foster, Richard. *Freedom of Simplicity*. Harper, 1981

Fox, Matthew. *The Coming of the Cosmic Christ*. Harper & Row, 1988

Freudenberger, C. Dean. *Food for Tomorrow?* Augsburg,

Freudenberger, C. Dean. *Global Dustbowl*. Augsburg, 1991

George, Susan. *A Fate Worse than Debt*. Grove Press, 1988

Global Songs #1 and 2 Fortress, 1996

Gonzales, Justo. *Faith and Wealth*. Harper and Row, 1990

Gonzales, Justo. *Mañana*. Abingdon, 1990

Gonzales, Justo, Justo and Gonzales, Catherine. *The Liberating Pulpit*. Abingdon, 1994

Graham, Katharine. *Personal History*. Vintage Books, 1998

Guitierrez, Gustavo. *A Theology of Liberation*. Orbis, 1973

Guitierrez, Gustavo. *We Drink from Our Own Wells*. Orbis, 1984

Hall, Douglas John. *Why Christian?* Augsburg, 1998

Harris, Marion. *Proclaim Jubilee* A Spirituality for the Twenty First Century. Westminister John Knox, 1996

Haugen, Gary A. *Good News About Injustice*. InterVarsity Press, 1999.

Haughey, John. *Virtue and Affluence*. Sheed L. Ward, 1997

Herzog, William II. *Jesus, Justice and the Reign of God*. Westminster John Knox, 2000

Herzog, William II. *Parables as Subversive Speech*. Westminster John Knox, 1994

Herschel, Abraham Joshua. *I Asked For Wonder*. Crossroads, 1998

Heyward, Carter. *Our Passion for Justice*. Pilgrim Press, 1984

Jackson, Wes. *Becoming Native to this Place*. University of Kentucky Press, 1994

Johnson, George S. *Critical Decisions in Following Jesus*. CSS Publishers, 1992

Johnson, George S. *Following Jesus* Small Group Study. Augsburg, 1995

Jones, E. Stanley. *The Reconstruction of the Church-On What Pattern*. Abingdon, 1970

Kavanaugh, John Francis. *Following Christ in a Consumer Society*. Orbis, 1981

Kraybill, Donald B. *The Upside Down Kingdom*. Herald Press, 1978

La Pierre, Dominique. *The City of Joy*. Warner Books, 1986

Lappe, Frances Moore. *Diet for a Small Planet*. Food First Books, 1975

Lappe, Frances Moore and Collins, Joseph. *World Hunger, Twelve Myths*. Food First Books 1986

Lappe, Frances Moore and Dubois, Martin Paul. *The Quickening of America*. Jossey- Bass Publishers, 1994

Marty, Martin. *Politics, Religion and the Common Good*. Jossey-Bass, 2000

Miranda, Jose. *Communism in the Bible*. Orbis, 1982

Miranda, Jose. *Marx and the Bible*. Orbis, 1974

Music From Taize. Collins Liturgical Press. Volumes I and II, 1986

Myers, Bryant. *Walking with the Poor*. Orbis/World Vision, 1999

Myers, Ched. *Binding the Strong Man*. A Political Reading of Mark's Gospel. Orbis, 1997

BIBLIOGRAPHY

Nelson-Pallmeyer, Jack. *Families Valued.* Parenting and Politics for the Good of all People. Friendship Press, 1996

Nolan, Albert. *Jesus Before Christianity.* Orbis, 1976

Nouwen, Henri. *Gracias.* Harper and Row, 1983

Ogden, Greg. *The New Reformation.* Zondervan, 1990

Peterson, Eugene H. *The Contemplative Pastor.* Eerdmans, 1989

Peterson, Eugene H. *Subversive Spirituality.* Eerdmans, 1997

Raheb, Mitri. *I Am a Palestinian Christian.* Fortress, 1995

Raines, Robert. *Creative Brooding.* Macmillan, 1966

Rasmussen, Larry. *Earth Community-Earth Ethics.* Orbis, 1996

Roberts, W. Dayton. *Patching God's Garment.* Enviornment and Mission in the 21st Century. MARC World Vision, 1994

Rohr, Richard. *Jesus Plan for the New World.* Sermon on the Mount. St. Anthony Press, 1996

Rohr, Richard. *Simplicity, The Art of Living.* Crossroads, 2000

Shaull, Richard. *Naming the Idols.* Meyer Stone Books, 1988

Sider, Ron. *Just Generosity.* Baker Books, 1999

Sider, Ron. *Rich Christians in an Age of Hunger.* Intervarsity, 1997

Simon, Arthur. *Christian Faith and Public Policy.* Eerdmans, 1987

Sine, Tom. *The Mustard Seed Versus McWorld.* Baker Books, 1999

Sobrino, Jon. *Christology at the Cross Roads.* Orbis, 1978

Sobrino, Jon. *The True Church and the Poor.* Orbis, 1984

Soelle, Dorothee. *The Arms Race Kills, Even Without War.* Fortress, 1983

Soelle, Dorothee. *Window of Vulnerability.* A Political Spirituality. Fortress, 1990

Soelle, Dorothee and Steffensky, Fulbert. *Not Just Yes and Amen.* Fortress, 1983

Songs of Faith from Around the World. Augsburg, 1996

Soros, George. *The Crisis of Global Capitalism.* Public Affairs, 1998

Tamez, Elsa. *Bible of the Oppressed.* Orbis, 1982

Taylor, John. *Enough Is Enough.* SCM Press, 1975

To Celebrate and *Simple Living 101.* Alternatives 800-821-6153

Wallis, Jim. *The Call to Conversion.* Harper & Row, 1981

Wallis, Jim. *Faith Works.* Random House, 2000

Weems, Renita. *Just a Sister Away.* LuraMedia, 1988

Wilcox, Fred, editor. *Disciples and Dissidents.* Haley, 2000.

Williams, Bill. *Naked Before God.* Moorehouse, 1998

Wink, Walter. *Engaging the Powers.* Fortress, 1992

Wink, Walter. *The Powers That Be.* Galilee Doubleday, 1998

Wuthnow, Robert. *The Crisis in the Church.* Oxford Press, 1997

Yoder, John Howard. *The Politics of Jesus.* Eerdmans, 1994

ABOUT THE AUTHOR

George S. Johnson, one of eight children born to George and Gladys Johnson, has served the church for more than 40 years. After graduation from Augustana College in Sioux Falls, South Dakota, he received his M.Div. and M.Th degrees from Luther Seminary in St. Paul, Minnesota and a D.Min. degree from the School of Theology in Claremont, California. In 1979-80 he did a year of graduate study at the Dag Hammarskjold Insttute in Uppsala, Sweden, sponsored by a Lutheran World Fedration grant.

Dr. Johnson served parishes in Lakewood, Long Beach, Pacifica and Tustin, California and White Bear Lake, Circle Pines and Cambridge, Minnesota. He has lectured at Umphumulo Seminary and Fort Hare University in South Africa as well as Gurukul Theological College in Madras, India and United Theological College in Harare, Zimbabwe. From 1987-93 he was adjunct professor at Luther Seminary teaching "Toward a Theology of Justice and Peace" and taught the same course at Fuller Seminary extension in Orange County, California.

From 1980-87 Johnson was the Director of the Hunger Program of the former American Lutheran Church when he traveled extensively internationally. He served as advisor to the Committee on Economic Justice for the Lutheran World Federation assembly in Budapest in 1984.

George is married to Vivian Elaine who is the co-creator of *Lifestories* and *Future Stories*, games of conversation and storytelling. They are parents of two daughters, Sonja Johnson-Egertson and Joy Wright, and have five grandchildren. Their son Todd died of cancer at the age of 15.

Other published works by George S. Johnson:

Following Jesus (Matthew 5 and Exodus 3), a Study Guide for Small Groups, Augsburg Fortress, 1995

How to Start Small Groups, And Keep Them Going (with other authors), Augsburg Fortress, 1995

Critical Decisions in Following Jesus, CSS Publishers, 1992

Evangelsim and the Poor, with Ana deGarcia, Augsburg Fortress, 1985

Articles: "Africa On Fire," "Zacchaeus 3-5-1," "Small Groups – A Quiet Revolution," "My Brother is Dying," "Rich Man – Poor Lazarus Bible Study" and a series of editorials called "Thoughts While Shaving."